Kenya Jacaranda
A Brixham Trawler

Edited by Bob Ferris

First published in Great Britain by
Rascal Books 2011

ISBN 978-0-9540344-3-6

www.kenyajacaranda.org

Printed and bound in Great Britain by:
stabur graphics limited
Unit 4
Deer Park Observatory
24 Deer Park Road
LONDON
SW19 3UA

Dedication

This book is dedicated to 'Steve' Stevens, without whose commitment the *Kenya Jacaranda* would surely have perished many years ago. Unashamedly, I mention the hours I spent transposing Dad's 100 or so pages of notes, typed on a manual Olivetti typewriter which punched out holes whenever an a, o or full stop were used. Sincere thanks to Bill Larkin who knocked the draft into some semblance of a book and to Bob Ferris my brother-in-law who, once enthused, pushed the project through to completion.

We have deliberately not mentioned many individuals by name as, inevitably, some would be missed out; those who have contributed to KJ know who they are and their participation is greatly appreciated.

There are inevitably some errors in this book; they are not deliberate and it is hoped that no-one is too offended. Any additional information or corrections can be communicated to me for inclusion in any reprint.

Roger Stevens

rogerstevens@kenyajacaranda.org

Arthur George "Steve" Stevens - a Biography

The history of the *Torbay Lass*, later renamed the *Kenya Jacaranda*, spans the years from 1923 to this day, and her whole history is an interesting one, but much of this book is written because of (or in spite of!) her management by the Bermondsey Sea Cadets from 1951 and the Mayflower Sail Training Trust (MSTS) from 1980 until 2007. There would be no story to be told were it not for Arthur George "Steve" Stevens. Steve was born in 1914 in Loughton, Essex, the son of the Police Station Sergeant. At the age of 16 he went to sea with the Merchant Navy and travelled the world, but in 1936 he followed his father into the Metropolitan Police.

In the early years of WWII he continued to patrol the streets of Bermondsey, but in 1942 he was freed from his status as a member of a Reserved Occupation to join the Royal Naval Volunteer Reserve (RNVR). He trained in Scotland as a Tank Landing Craft commander and spent the rest of the war afloat and in command of a small flotilla of craft, continuing after the War as a RNVR officer involved in mine clearance until 1948. In his heart, Steve was always a sailor, albeit he returned to the Police and served at Tower Bridge Police Station as a Constable until his retirement in 1966. He devoted as much time as he possibly could on his beloved *Kenya Jacaranda* - he always referred to her as his mistress and he loved her dearly.

When he died in 2008, aged 94, the *Kenya Jacaranda* was in sad decline. She was still at Tilbury Dock but needed a lot of work, which of course meant she needed the one thing that she didn't have - money. However, his family and friends decided that the most fitting tribute they could pay to Steve was to scatter his ashes from the *Kenya Jacaranda* into the Thames. That was not to prove as simple as it sounds.

On Saturday 16 August 2008 his family and friends assembled aboard and, for the last time, the Blue Ensign was raised, a former Naval officer being aboard. The engines were started and the ship moved slowly away from her berth. However, something was amiss - she was not making way as she should and it was quickly established that this was due to the amount of algae that had accumulated on her hull; she had been stationary at her moorings for a long time. A trip around the Dock was called for to see if joining the stream was viable.

As far as power was concerned the Skipper decided that we had sufficient, but then another problem - or, more correctly, two more problems - presented themselves: both engines were overheating. A crew member despatched to the engine room reported that the water pumps were not doing their job of cooling the engines properly but a little ingenuity and the judicious use of a hosepipe would suffice as a short fix. Thus, the decision was made - we were going out.

The Lock staff were acquainted with the problems and agreed to leave the Lock gates open while we made a dash for the stream, despatched Steve's ashes to forever roam the Seven Seas, and returned. Thus, with the two Tilbury Dock policemen standing to attention and the Blue Ensign fluttering in the wind, we made our cautious way out.

Having reached the Thames a few words were said in tribute to Steve, his mortal remains were consigned to the Thames, the Blue Ensign was lowered and replaced with the Red Ensign and we turned back. An element of humour presented itself at this moment - the crew member who had been minding the engines poked his head out of the engine room hatch and asked, "When are we doing it?". Sadly, he was too late but had provided a valuable role that had allowed it to happen.

The story of the *Kenya Jacaranda* is a fascinating one and continues to be so, but common elements repeat themselves - accidents, misadventures and high drama feature large in the story of Steve's reign as her Master. It was only fitting that should be the case on his last day aboard.

THE KENYA JACARANDA

THE EARLY YEARS

An introduction by Bill Larkin

The *Kenya Jacaranda* (KJ) is a Brixham Trawler. She was and is a heavily built workboat and is a living reminder of our great sailing heritage. Such trawlers were built to a design that evolved over the years. The basic pattern was the same, but the most appealing aesthetic feature of the KJ is her long and dramatic counter. In the 1920s there were over 200 in Brixham, a relatively small port. There are now but nine: Pilgrim, Leader, Provident, Regard, Vigilance, Ethel (in Germany), Deodar (in Sweden), Iris (in Norway) and the *Kenya Jacaranda*.

Kenya Jacaranda was built by R Jackman & Sons in 1923 and fished out of Brixham until 1935. She was first called " *Torbay Lass*", with the registered fishing number BM163. She is a gaff rigged ketch and her vital statistics are: 69 ft long without the bowsprit, an 18ft 8ins beam, a registered tonnage of 31.1 tons and a total weight of 85 tons.

Of course, when built these boats had no engines - Brixham trawlers were sailing boats and they would sail in and out of harbour, a somewhat amazing feat as there could be 200 - 300 boats packed together inside the mole. They could also be towed in and out of harbour by a steam pinnace and carried sweeps [oars] to allow the crew to manoeuvre them by rowing.

The strength of the construction of the boat was necessary to tow the heavy trawl. This was a tapering tarred rope bag, open at the top and reducing in size to the narrower part. It was supported and pulled over a substantial spar called a beam, perhaps 40 feet long, which explains why these ships were often called "beam trawlers".

The First Owner

Alf Lovis was the first owner and Skipper of the *Torbay Lass* and he must have been a remarkable seaman, as the opening paragraphs of Steve's Story will demonstrate.

Alf was also a popular man. As Skipper he raced *Torbay Lass* and in 1936 won *"the Brixham Trawler Race"* a perpetual challenge cup presented by King George V. The speed of the boats was and is astounding; in 1929 the *average* speed was 13.9 knots. The maximum speed can only be imagined and again it is a tribute to Alf Lovis that they won such a prestigious cup.

[Amazingly, you can actually see this on YouTube - the link is http://www.youtube.com/watch?v=2aKlhD7FrpU].

All of these boats are very beautiful and a gorgeous sight, particularly so when viewed from Torquay. It is said that *Torbay Lass* was the subject of the well known song *"Red Sails in the Sunset"*. Written by Jimmy Kennedy, with music by Hugh Williams, this song has been recorded by many well known singers and legend has it that it was composed while looking at her sailing into the sunset across Torbay towards Brixham.

It must have been a very sad day when Alf put his boat *Torbay Lass* up for sale. He had at least one son and the name Lovis abounds in Brixham today. Certainly the boat was in good condition but, unlike many others that were literally beached, she quickly found a new owner.

The Second Owner

The next owner was Harry Edward Bradshaw, of Grove Farm House, Southend Road, Rainham. On the British Registration the date of ownership is given as 15 June 1939, but Brixham Heritage gives the date as 11 October 1938. It seems that the earlier date is the correct one as we know from the comprehensive diaries of her third owner, Mrs Genesta Long, that a substantial reformation took place before WWII. He probably took some time to register the change of ownership. [Genesta was born in 1899 and died in 1990. She was born Genesta Heath and married three times. Her married names were Farquhar, Long and Lady Claud Hamilton respectively.]

Certainly he was responsible for the boat being converted into a pleasure yacht. The engines were installed and alterations to the layout were substantial. At this moment, in 2004, there are two cabins below by the companionway and then a galley with a further bulkhead forward; this is possibly the original layout. All the other partitions have been removed as part of the rebuilding that has taken place.

The alterations were substantial as a *wheel-house* was constructed and a deck area was glazed - this has been changed to a traditional skylight. Toilets and a galley were installed and the bottom was sheaved in copper.

This work must have taken at least three months to be carried out and therefore it would have been Spring 1939 before any cruising could take place. Beyond this we have no certain information about the *Torbay Lass* until 1944 when without doubt she was in Lowestoft. However, Stanley Earl of the Port of Lowestoft Research Society, who very helpfully tried to find some records of her during this period, recently heard from a colleague a story that I have heard before; namely that Harry Bradshaw went on a cruise to Scotland.

This is certainly possible within the time period. War was pending and on the way back south he was stopped by the Royal Navy and advised to go into Hull. Harry Bradshaw then decided to press further south and went into Lowestoft. Many fishing boats were in Lowestoft during this period and were used as floating accommodation for officers of the Royal Navy, or for holding barrage balloons. The boats were not only on Lake Lothing, which is part of the harbour, but they were also crowded on Oulton Broad, which is entered from the harbour. This seems likely as the interior would have been finished to a higher standard than a normal workboat.

The Third Owner

The British Registry shows that Mrs Genesta Long became the owner of *Torbay Lass* on 29 September 1944, having bought her from Harry Bradshaw. Fortunately she kept a diary throughout her later life, a synopsis of which was edited by her and published in 1986 as "*A Stone's Throw*" and so we are in the excellent position of being able to have a description of the boat at that time.

She was born into a very wealthy family who owned Anstey Grange in Surrey and neighbouring properties called Kitlands and Moorhurst. Her father was an extremely wealthy and distinguished man. Although he owned an insurance company there was a great naval tradition in the family and indeed he would have joined the Navy had it not been that he was slightly deaf. In Victorian times her grandfather had been responsible for fighting slave traders in the Indian Ocean and the Persian Gulf. During WWI two uncles were knighted: both were Commanders in Chief in Portsmouth, one of the Navy and the other of the Army. This naval tradition much influenced Genesta as she clearly loved sailing; her diary gives descriptions of sailing in the Solent and later in the Middle East.

It would be wrong to gloss over her early life as it was so different from that of her peers. She was brave to the point of foolhardiness. A nurse during WWI, she then developed a passion for adventurous and solitary expeditions into wild and unexplored parts of the world. Part of this adventurous life led her to Kenya where she went many times on safari; she would stay up all night waiting to shoot elephants or wild dogs while the male hunters were all safely in camp. These solitary expeditions went on throughout her life and she bought a farm in Kenya which has a lake on the shores of Lake Nakuro with a massive flock of flamingos. The lake is now very well known and is often seen on television and in films. On this farm she entertained many important people, including the Duke of Windsor.

One must not give the impression of a solitary, humourless person; in fact she loved entertaining and tells a good story of one party which became rather disorderly. A young man carrying a bush knife was forcibly put into a large chest by his friends; they locked it and happily returned to the party. He kicked and shouted but nobody took any notice. A young lady, slightly the worse for drink, sat down on the lid, whereupon the young fellow again kicked and shouted, but she was oblivious. He then took his bush knife which was incredibly sharp and drove it upwards. The young lady ran screaming through the house with blood pouring all over the place. The hostess took the young lady to a bedroom and gave her an aspirin, some lint and sticking plaster and a mirror. In the morning the young lady was found fast asleep with the sticking plaster and lint carefully stuck onto the mirror

During these years Genesta became a part-time correspondent for the Daily Telegraph and went to Spain during the Spanish Civil War. One of her stories describes standing on a bridge on the French border watching the fighting and not sheltering when the bullets were close; indeed she was waving to the fighters. She describes this period as one of the most exciting of her life. Later she went to Germany and Eastern Europe and describes the dreadful experience of the Jews at the hands of the Nazis. Later, just before the beginning of WWII, she went to Greece where, with friends, she took a small motor boat all the way to Vigo in Portugal. They were advised that they could be sunk by U Boats so they kept within the three mile limit. One morning in harbour they found themselves surrounded by German merchant vessels. A ship's boat came alongside with a grim faced crew, but Genesta and the skipper showed their disrespect by having breakfast on deck in their pyjamas.

During WWII she was a driver for the Women's Royal Voluntary Service (WRVS) in Dover and then Folkestone, where she describes honestly her fear induced by the V1 and V2 rockets. At this time she was introduced to Lord Claud Hamilton, an officer in the Irish Guards, and they kept up a correspondence when he went to France as part of the D Day landings. It was during this period that Genesta saw *Torbay Lass*: the following is from her diary.

".... but the Folkestone days had led me to one marvellous thing - to a lovely ship, my future home. Through a shipbuilder at Hastings I heard of a Brixham Trawler at Lowestoft, and went up there post-haste to see what I could find. And there she lay, the *Torbay Lass*, the perfect craft for me. Oak built, converted to a yacht and ketch rigged, she has a big saloon aft with a stove in it, four big double berth cabins, two lavatories, a big roomy fo'c'sle, and a deck house. She is quite spacious - seventy foot long, eighteen wide, and with an eight foot six draft. It was a case of love at first sight, and after a little manoeuvring with my dear bank manager I was able to buy the boat for £2,000. This is less than her value, and when she is fitted out for sea she will be worth at least double that. Now I have something definite and stable to look forward to after the War".

However, Genesta's life was about to change; first her mother died and left her the family home at Moorhurst. Again to quote: "I inherited Moorhurst, a sixteenth century manor house which had been in my family for over 150 years. I had a home, servants, a garden and plenty of space for me and my friends and my dogs".

Then, in 1946, her life changed even more; Lord Claud returned from the War and she became Lady Claud Hamilton, marrying a man who was distinguished in his own right and very well connected. His uncle was Lord Alexander of Tunis, said by many to be the finest soldier since Wellington. His family home is Baron's Court, a substantial Georgian mansion in Northern Ireland. Above all he shared Lady Genesta's passion for travel.

They lived a great deal of their lives in Kenya, building a very respected herd of cattle and interspersed with much adventure. The Mau Mau campaign was taking place at this time and they spent many nights with revolvers under the pillows.

Sailing remained part of their lives. Genesta gives a lovely description of the Indian Ocean while sailing on a friend's yacht:

"The first night stop was in a creek called Shimoni, where once the Masai used to raid right down to the shore. Next morning we crept out of the creek, very early and quietly under a pale gold sky and sailed south for Pemba. In the evening we entered a fairyland bay. There we lay for the night, on a star-shimmering sea under a star-flecked sky, dreaming of darkest, loneliest Africa".

Lord and Lady Claud Hamilton were now very much part of the aristocracy. They took part in the Coronation and his niece was one of the six Ladies-in-Waiting to the Queen. They would have had little time for sailing *Torbay Lass*.

A lovely story is told when they were in a box having lunch at Goodwood. Princess Margaret came in and, being royalty, nobody could sit down until she did. The Princess thoroughly enjoyed herself and stayed for hours. Lady Genesta was none too happy and had indigestion from standing up for so long.

Lady Genesta rarely if ever sailed *Torbay Lass* but nevertheless, due to her ties with Kenya, she had the name changed to *Kenya Jacaranda*. Regretfully Lady Genesta had a full social life and had to contemplate selling her boat. However, at a dinner party she talked to Captain R G Bowes Lyon, a distinguished naval officer and cousin to the Queen Mother, and Commanding Officer of a group of Sea Cadets. Very kindly Lady Genesta agreed to allow the use of *Kenya Jacaranda* by these young people.

The officer of the local platoon was "Steve" Stevens who for many years devoted his life and energies to the successful running of the ship as a training vessel for over 7,000 youngsters. Ultimately ownership was passed to Steve Stevens and Peter Harding, at first under the management of the Sea Cadets and later the Mayflower Sail Training Society.

STEVE'S STORY

Chapter 1 - The Kenya Jacaranda arrives

Kenya Jacaranda was launched from Jackman's Yard in Brixham in 1923 as *Torbay Lass*. She was ketch-rigged, of 32 tons net register, 69ft. on the waterline and was one of the last of a long line of Brixham sailing trawlers. She had no engines and worked the western ocean fishing grounds, a very hard school indeed.

She was built to sail, and to sail hard; working a massive beam trawl called for plenty of power. This was demonstrated very well on Saturday May 18 1935, when she carved a niche for herself in maritime history. Having been fishing off Land's End, she had spent a night hove to in gale force northerly winds off Wolf Rock light. She sighted a 3-masted schooner flying distress signals and with only a couple of makeshift sails hoisted.

The ship was the Appledore-owned auxiliary schooner, the *Welcome*, of 119 tons, bound from Newport to Plymouth with coal. The previous afternoon she had fouled her propeller with a rope, putting the engine out of action, and although she had managed to clear the Longships it cost her most of her canvas as sail after sail blew out.

She was wallowing in heavy seas east of Wolf Rock when *Torbay Lass* ranged alongside at 0700 and put a tow aboard. Under sail alone, *Torbay Lass* towed her, heavy with 200 tons of coal, with only a makeshift trysail on her mainmast and a fore staysail to help. They sailed into Newlyn, reaching there at 1930, after a tow of over 12 hours; not only into Newlyn, but into history, with her and her skipper Mr Alfred Lovis being partners in the last salvage tow under sail.

Soon after this she was, with many of her sisters, literally put on the beach as it was no longer possible for them to compete with the power vessels that were taking over all round the coast. Some of them were broken up, some were sold (although they had little scrap value) and some were just stripped of anything worthwhile and run ashore to rot. *Torbay Lass* was luckier than most as she was purchased by a Kenyan landowner, Lady Claud Hamilton. Her Ladyship installed two Kelvin petrol-paraffin (PP) engines, copper sheathed her, built cabins and a bathroom below decks and put a wheelhouse and a dog house aft of her mainmast. Once wheel steering had replaced the tiller she became a yacht!

In 1936 she made a cruise to the Mediterranean, returning home to spend some time in Scottish waters. In 1939 she was still there, but with the imminence of hostilities with Germany in the offing the owner tried to get her back to the south coast. However, the Royal Navy intercepted her and put her into Lowestoft, where she remained for the duration. Even the Navy, hard put to as they were for anything that floated, could not think of a use for her apart from as a target!

After the war she was returned to her owner and brought south to the Hamble, but her owner had by now become disenchanted with her and in the event never used her again. Most of her gear was taken ashore and she was put up for sale at an asking price of £3,000, but there were no takers.

In 1947 I was demobbed from the Royal Navy and returned to my pre-war job, the Metropolitan Police. I returned to Tower Bridge Police Station and almost straight away became involved in the Sea Cadet Unit in Bermondsey, which had its H.Q. in a school in Tower Bridge Road. The President of the Unit was Captain R.J. Bowes-Lyon, MVO, RN, a name to conjure with. The Commanding Officer was a civilian, really a caretaker for the war years, and he left very shortly afterwards; I was then appointed First Lieutenant.

Shortly after that the new Commanding Officer, who worked for a printing firm in the city, resigned. At that time a working week included Saturday and he was told by a colleague in the firm that the Managing Director had been asking for him on the Saturday morning. On being told that he was "playing with his boat", he was heard to say that if "playing with his boat was more important than his job there was no more to be said". That meant that, in a matter of months, I went from bottom to top and became C.O.

The Unit had a 112ft Fairmile ex-Admiralty motor torpedo boat, minus engines. This was moored in the Surrey Commercial Docks and we quickly realised that this was a much better venue for a Sea Cadet Unit than a school. Everything we used in the school had to be stowed away afterwards, and stowage space was at a premium. We had to take many of the things home after every parade and bring them back for the next one; this meant that things got mislaid and it was the cause of many upsets.

One parade night, by courtesy of Tower Bridge, Deptford and Southwark police utility vans(!), we vacated the school and moved into the Surrey Docks; this proved to be one of the best things we ever did. In those days there was a lot of sympathy for cadet forces, especially for Sea Cadets in a riparian borough. We already had a 27ft Montague Whaler and we managed to supplement it with a ship's 44 man lifeboat, fitted with a dipping lug sail. Money was scarce but we managed to raise a lot for the Unit by diverse means. Moreover, we had in the docks the companies Furness Withy, Harland & Wolff and Cunard; many were the useful bits and bobs that came our way.

We later got the use of a semi-underground air-raid shelter which was located in the docks, but the Port of London Authority (PLA) disclaimed all knowledge of it and said that it belonged to Bermondsey Borough Council; they in turn said that it was the property of the 'Ministry'; my question "The Ministry of what?" never received an answer. On the Unit Committee we had the Borough Treasurer for our own cash, and the Borough Engineer. We also had the Surrey Harbour Master, with the added presence of the Chief Inspector of the P.L.A. Police not going amiss.

Later we cleared all the earth from the top of the shelter because the roof leaked and gave it two coats of hot tar. We also enlarged the hole through the roof and installed a large coal burning stove. The blast walls at each end and in the middle were reinforced concrete 15 inches thick, which made it very difficult to get anything large inside. We did manage, by days of constant hammering, to get out a section sufficient for us to get oars inside and that section became a boat store.

When, at a committee meeting a few months later, I told the committee what we had done, the Borough Engineer said he did not think it possible to go through 12 inches of concrete roof. When I told him the roof was only 2 inches thick he went a very queer colour, even more so when I took him over to the shelter and drove a pick axe clean through at one hit. I realised afterwards that, as he had been in his post during the war, perhaps the contractor had cheated a bit with his concreting. I did not say anything further to him on the subject but I thought what a good thing it was that the occupants of that shelter during the raids were not aware that there was literally nothing between them and the outside world.

In May 1951 I had a telephone call from the President. Unlike many presidents of sea cadet units, we never considered him to be just a name as he took a such great interest in the Unit and could always be relied on to support any function. On this occasion he said that he had been at a dinner recently and had been introduced to Lady Claud Hamilton. She had remarked, possibly because of his rank, that she owned a Brixham sailing trawler and was trying to sell it, but was not having much success. He had suggested to her that she let a Sea Cadet Unit have it on a peppercorn rent. They would benefit with access to an actual ship and she might benefit in as much as they would keep it running and possible buyers could see it in a more favourable light than swinging round a buoy.

She jumped at the idea; when he said he was connected with a Unit it was, as far as she was concerned, all systems go. He had told her that he would talk it over with the committee and staff and would let her know the outcome. What did I think? Well, first I thought, "What's a Brixham trawler?"; he did not know for sure, but what was there to lose? "Only our lives," I thought, but I didn't know him well enough at that stage to say it! Anyway, it was agreed that we had nothing, apart from my mental reservation, to lose, and an appointment was made for a deputation from the Unit to go and have a look.

We went to Bursledon on the Hamble a week or two later where we met the manager of the yard and were taken in a rowing boat to see the ship. At that state of the tide, just after low water, she was lying on her side in a mud berth; rowing around her she looked immense. We had been told that there were two engines, but the sight of two tiny propellers at the stern, almost touching the hull, gave us cause to wonder exactly what kind of engines they were.

There was a miscellany of wires, ropes and chains on and around the deck although the bo'sun of the yard told us that 'most of the gear' had been taken ashore.

We returned to the yard and arranged to come back at high water, retiring to a local establishment that catered for indigent seafarers in a very thoughtful mood. Little was said until we actually got on board and we were shown round above and below deck. After five years in the Merchant Service, and five more in the Royal Navy, I was not entirely ignorant of things maritime, but never ever had I seen anything like her.

The five years that she had spent closed right down and neglected had left their mark; there were signs of rot in several places, paint had flaked off, varnish was white and she looked a poor raddled old lady. The main sheet (I knew that it was the bottom back end of the mainsail) was made up of two to three sheave blocks, rove off with 3" rope, and there was no way that I could envisage youngsters coping with that sort of gear. The bo'sun agreed that "there was a fair bit to do" but opined that it was well worth it. He obviously wanted to see the back, or rather the stern, of her.

The Kelvin engines were hand-started jobs. They started on petrol and ran until they were hot, at which stage they could be turned over to run on paraffin, then known as TVO, which was short for Tractor Vaporising Oil. There was a 30 gallon petrol tank let into the deck amidships, with a gravity feed to the engine room. There were two brass wheels on a bracket in the wheel-house, each connected to an engine by sprockets and bicycle chain. Later on we fitted a drip tray beneath each to catch knuckles.

The electrics consisted of a 12 volt car battery in the engine room. There was a single cylinder engine with a big flywheel and a slip belt, which on one side charged the battery via a car dynamo nailed to the ship's side and on the other ran a bilge pump. Cooking was done by paraffin stove with four banks of wicks, each about the size of a pencil, with each bank having ten wicks. When this ran out of paraffin and the wicks had to be trimmed it didn't take hours, it took days!; we only let it go dry *once*.

There was a line of cabins on either side, in what would have been the fish hold. A sea toilet was fitted in the foc'sle and a Blake's 'Victory' sea toilet was on the starboard side, obviously one of the owner's perks! A small galley with a sink and little else was on the other side; even Nelson would have thought it spartan!

Against my judgment the committee decided that we should give her a month's trial. I do not think that anybody ever gave the matter of returning her to Bursledon from London much thought, and in the event the proposition never arose. In due course, when we were told the sails were 'bent on' and the 'rest of the gear' was put aboard, the collection party went to the Hamble and took her away on high water. The engineer was an ex sub-mariner and not only had he never heard of a Kelvin PP, he had never given the possibility of hand starting a four cylinder engine much consideration. The flow of invective that came from the engine room hatch aroused the admiration and envy of all who heard it, although in order to lessen the impact on the natives we closed the engine room hatch.

When the engines had been started and appeared to be running smoothly we slipped the buoy and crept very gingerly into the stream. Thinking in terms of single flag hoists we had a quick run through the possibilities. "Keep clear of me I am manoeuvring with difficulty" appeared to meet the case, with "Keep out of my way, I cannot get out of yours" was also a distinct possibility as a second choice. As a last resort there was "I require assistance" and "I require a tug" or "I am disabled, communicate with me". Someone with a fine sense of occasion said "Why not put them all up?"

Benign Providence must have been looking out for us that day, although it was only later that we appreciated how lucky we had been. Running with the tide in a narrow channel there was only one way we could have stopped, and that would have been to drop the anchor and bring all of our worry beads into play. We switched over to T.V.O. and prayed, but there was no noticeable difference in the engine notes and we finally reached the Solent proper. Up to that time we had disregarded the mass of ropes and wires that abounded, but now we had the chance to sort some of them out. As a general rule, if we pulled on one end and nothing happened at the other, that particular rope was superfluous.

Sorting out the sails we found that the smallest one, right at the front, was a reasonably easy one to hoist and the ropes for doing this were attached to it. There were bent wires holding it to the forestay (I knew that one) and up it went. Again, good fortune was with us; the wind was going the same way as we were and the sail blew out nicely. Luckily, again, there was not too much of it, just enough to whet our appetites. The next sail in size was right at the back. This was rather different, with a pole at top and bottom; the lifting gear was a pulley on a smaller mast on the top pole. After one or two false starts we got that one up too and as soon as we realised that we had to untie the bottom pole the whole sail swung out to the side and it too, filled with wind.

We were sailing!

The gods really did smile on us, not only on that day but also on the following ones. The wind was in our favour, being not too strong but just strong enough to show what the ship was capable of. The ship herself seemed to want us to succeed; she must have known that we were all on trial, ship and crew alike. We managed, after four abortive attempts, to get the mainsail up. It was far from right and some of the other "proper" sailors (albeit sailors in much smaller boats) that we encountered must have thought we were splicing the mainbrace hourly; they certainly gave us a wide berth.

With (what we knew later to be) fore, main and mizzen up, after getting assurance from the engine room that the engines could be re-started, they were turned off. From that moment she was ours and we were hers. That has endured for over 40 years.

On Sunday June 10 1951 we got her into the Thames and up-river to the Surrey Docks, where we berthed her alongside our motor launch and took stock. Rot, both wet and dry, was rampant; in several places the deck, which should have been 2 ½" thick, was down to under an inch. Additionally there was not a sound rope in her. The first serious thing that happened was the mizzen mast one day started to lean forward from deck level but we managed to get the sail down and to secure the mast until we returned. As this obviously needed replacing, we managed to get hold of a second hand spar, but it still cost us £125 to get it stepped and that was just for starters.

From time to time prospective owners would come down by appointment after a 'phone call from either the owner or the broker. Most of them had little idea of what a Brixham trawler was and she did not appeal to the usual run of yachtsmen. In the event of them showing any interest in her I knew of several places where I could run a 6 inch knife into an apparently solid oak beam, pointing out that there were one or two soft places here and there, and that was usually sufficient to ensure their departure.

The interior layout was most unhelpful to us as we wanted open space rather than cabins. Having written to her Ladyship asking if we could remove them, she agreed, so with a lot of effort we cleared the interior right out and made bunks against the ship's sides, which proved to be a much better arrangement.

Equally, the cooking arrangements were far from ideal, but I was very loath to install any form of gas facilities as the combination of boys, a wooden ship, thirty gallons of petrol and Calor gas was rather too much of a hazard! We persevered with the paraffin cooker, but used to boil a kettle on deck with a Primus stove, surrounded by boxes to form a wind break; it was a very austere ship.

Chapter 2 - The Early Years

For the first two years we did little more than run up and down the river, firstly on day trips and then for weekends to Southend. The engines were always a source of trouble, starting well enough on petrol, but both obviously preferring running on that than T.V.O., as they would frequently stop as soon as they were changed over.

We tried changing one engine at a time so that we were not left without a form of propulsion other than the sails. Often it worked, with us running one on petrol and the other on T.V.O. Everything would appear to be in our favour until we changed the second one over to T.V.O., which would then give a cough and stop. This invariably set up a sympathetic reaction in the first one which would also stop, leaving us usually in the middle of the river or some similar place where we were in everybody's way.

It became obvious that two new or different engines would have to be found somewhere, but where? New ones bought in the ordinary way (i.e. for the full market price!) were right out of the question, so the only thing we could do was to set up an engine fund, diverting any cash that we could raise in that direction.

In 1960 a combined operation involving 90 Royal Marines was set up including in part a sea trip to Calais with Sea Cadets not being on the agenda. The then London Area Officer, Captain Walter Scott R.N., heard about this and said (knowing him, with a lordly wave of the hand) "The Sea Cadets will supply the sea transport".

At that time there were several ex M.F.V.s (Motor Fishing Vessels, maids-of-all-work) in the Navy; they were used as NAAFI transport, Libertymen, Shore Patrols, Balloon Handlers, etc. etc.; in short, anything that did not involve sea fighting. At the end of the war there was a plenitude of these vessels, which had been built for the duration only, although the majority of them lasted for many years afterwards. Some were given to the Sea Cadets and Captain Scott had five in the London area; these were to be the sea transport. Apparently, when someone had said; "What about the *Kenya*

Jacaranda?" he was reputed to have replied, "We don't want that thing". In the event, all five of the M.F.V.s C.O.s opted out for one reason or another, and the deputy Area Officer rang me one day and told me this story. He said that the London Area Office wanted more than anything to be able to have at least a token presence, and could *Kenya Jacaranda* help?

At the next Unit meeting I told the lads this and said that I wanted, above all else, to be able to wipe Walter Scott's eye; we all agreed.

On July 9 1960 we loaded 29 Royal Marines, with all their gear, at Sheerness and duly dropped them in Calais. We left at 1300 and put them ashore at 1715, with a promise to collect them in 14 days.

On July 23 we got into Calais harbour at 0400 and waited for our Marines. At 1100 we were told to move the ship to another berth and a leading hand from Dover Unit dropped the stern line overboard, promptly fouling the port screw. We did not clear it until 1320 and at 1400 we took 35 Royal Marines aboard, again with all their gear. Had we had a Plimsoll Line we would have had to have used a skin diver to read it.

At 1545 we cleared the harbour entrance, and very soon afterwards the port engine gave notice that it was not going to be a party. Very luckily the wind was fair and we crossed on one engine and all sail. It was a very bumpy trip and almost all the Marines and some of the crew were very sick. I don't know where they all managed to fit in, but they did.

Arriving at Dover, we still did not have any working radio communication. When we got into the outer harbour, the Eastern entrance, we expected to be sent into the Western Arm, but we were told by Aldis lamp to berth in the Camber, the most easterly part of Dover harbour.

Unfortunately it was low water and, as the top of the mainmast was just level with the breakwater, the poor Marines had to climb about 70 feet up a vertical ladder hauling their kit up behind them on heaving lines. When three Customs officers came along and asked whether we had cleared Customs I said that the Marines were on their way to do it, but we were staying on board. This was that once in a while when Customs were human; they turned away and left them to it. It is possible that the sight of a Royal Marine in a very dishevelled state, trying the point of his bayonet while he was looking at them, may have had something to do with it; whatever the reason it was the fastest Custom clearance that we ever had.

Another record had been set; it was most certainly the last time that Royal Marines went into action under sail, even if only in fun. It was learning to swim by going off the deep end, but we learned a lot from it and in the long run it stood us in good stead. It was a long time however, before Captain Walter Scott would go to Bermondsey.

By 1961 we were beginning to really get the feel for her and we extended our range to Dover. We were berthed in the Wellington Dock and made the acquaintance of a Royal Naval party who were removing the last of the block-ships that had been put down at the Western entrance for the duration of the war. They had things very well organised, the duty watch in the morning checking the lobster pots, removing the denizens and replacing the empty pots for the evening watch to check. We had the freshest lobsters ever! They were very kind to us in many ways, although they were not blessed with any Naval stores which were of much use to us.

We found that, whenever we came across one of H.M.'s ships in port, they would help us in any way they could; paint, rope, canvas, deck scrubbers, wires, we always wanted something and seldom had to create a precedent and buy it!

In 1962 we made Ostend for the first time and there made many friends, some of whom we are still in contact with to this day. The naval base provided showers whenever we wanted them, as well as fresh bread and milk, and if we ever had a problem that called for the services of a workshop it was never refused. On our first visit to Ostend, when one of the engine heads started to leak we took it off and got it welded in the workshop; a little help is better than a lot of pity.

For several years from then on, Ostend was our venue for the August Bank Holiday week. It was an ideal cruise, and although preparations for it took up many hours the Cadets got a lot from it. Naval Authorities had tightened up and we had to notify the Commander-in-Chief Portsmouth (C in C (P)) of our times of departure and arrival, although we never found out why we had to notify Portsmouth when there was a Naval Command at Chatham, but there it was.

The 1963 cruise started with the first night at anchor at Sheerness, then over to Ostend on Sunday morning, with a 0500 departure time. By 1030 we were at the Tongue Lightship, the wind was foul and against us and the ship was pitching and rolling to an almost alarming extent. At 150 we altered course 180 degrees and, shutting off the engines, ran back to Sheerness under sail; it was hard to realise that it was the same stretch of water. The old old story, wind against tide, was the bane of sailing anywhere in the Thames estuary. We left again at 0800 on Monday and finally arrived in Ostend at 1140 on Tuesday. The return run started at midnight on Saturday and ended at 2010 that day. Those lads certainly got some sea time in, with us finally berthed in the Surrey Docks at 1500.

The next year, 1964, saw us in Calais and Boulogne for a long weekend, and then back to Ostend again in August. Instead of sailing for home on Thursday, we were told by a runner from the Consul's office that we were not to sail on account of gale warnings, with the same expected on Friday and Saturday. On Saturday two Cadets from Deptford Unit disappeared and, not having returned, were later seen hitch-hiking out of Ostend. As the Consul's office was closed their absence was reported to both Ostend Police and the British Military Attaché in Brussels.

The two lads were still missing on Sunday, and although the conditions were still bad in the morning it eased off in the afternoon and we decided to have a go at getting back with a night run. We informed Portsmouth and having got their blessing sailed at 1700, but conditions were still so bad when we got away from the coast that we returned to harbour, only to find a reception committee consisting of our two missing Cadets. We informed the police, who had reports of the two in different localities. They knew that we had several police officers in the Unit, and they asked me what I wanted to be done with them. Having told them that a few hours in a cell might have a salutary effect and not do any harm, the officer I spoke to said, "We'll put the frightening irons into them".

A few minutes later a Police Jeep, with two massive Belgian Policemen aboard, stopped at the gangway. Once the two miscreants they asked for were produced they were promptly handcuffed to a rail in the jeep and driven away, looking distinctly apprehensive. We finally left at 0630 the following morning, Monday, after our two very chastened offenders had been put back on board at 0600 by the police. This time we made it, although it was another long drag, and got Lloyd's station on the end of Southend Pier to notify Portsmouth that we were back. We anchored for the night and left at 0600 next day, Tuesday, berthing in Surrey Docks at 1230.

In 1965, August Bank Holiday saw us again in Ostend. By now we had made friends with, firstly, Paulette, a blond lady who worked in one of the dockside café s. She used to bring milk and bread to us every morning. The café was owned by her brother-in-law, Henri, who had been a ship's engineer but had swallowed the anchor and come ashore. He appeared to be on a diet composed of cognac in as many forms as possible. His brother Roger was Paulette's husband, and was an engineer on the Belgian mail boats, running to and from Dover. His duties were very erratic, but when he came in at about midnight he would collect his wife and often we would wander round Ostend with them, usually for a meal as well.

The weather was atrocious, with gale force winds almost every day; there was no question of leaving. In the adult crew there were three serving policemen: myself, a Thames Division Sergeant from Wapping and another P.C. from Kennington. He and I joined the Navy together at Collingwood where we received our initial training, after which he went to HMS King Alfred at Brighton and I went to Combined Ops. in Troon. We were all due back on duty on Monday, but when it became obvious that there was no way we would make it the Thames Sergeant volunteered to go back on the mail boat, taking the nominal list of the crew and informing all of the parents that little Willy etc. would be coming home as soon as possible. He also got in touch with the Superintendents at Tower Bridge and Kennington.

Rather to our surprise he came back on the Tuesday, having first found out that we were not en route, and we began to consider taking all hands back on the mail boat. Normally we carried enough tinned food to last us a whole trip, and only had to buy fresh food, but by this time we were down to rock bottom and were buying food ashore. In consequence the exchequer was getting thin. Paulette, who of course knew our position, suggested that Roger might be able to suggest something and said he would be in by 0100. Whilst we were waiting most of the Cadets came along on their way aboard, but seeing us in the café came in and asked what the position was. They, too, were getting very low on francs. Thus Paulette took one of their uniform caps and went round the café for funds for "les petit matelots de la Marine Brittanique" and in no time at all they were far more in funds than we were!

Roger came ashore at just about midnight, and called out, "Steve - still here?" I told him that we would have to go back on the mailboat but that it was doubtful if we had sufficient funds. Without a second's hesitation he said, reaching into his pocket, " How much do you want? Five thousand francs? Ten thousand?"

To think that anybody would be willing to loan such a sum at the drop of a hat to someone who was little more than a casual acquaintance was quite something. However, I told him I was hoping he might be able to suggest the right person to approach with a view to being treated as stranded British Seamen. He said; "You must see Commandant Kesteloot and tell him you are attached to the Royal Navy. If he will not help you, tell him you will ring Brussels". I did not really fancy my chance saying a thing like that but I had to give it a try.

The next morning, with my last clean shirt on, I went to the office and asked for the Commandant. I told him that I was the Captain of *Kenya Jacaranda*, that we were storm bound and could not wait any longer for a break in the weather, and that we did not have sufficient funds to pay. He said, "Then you cannot go" intimating that any fool could work that out. Then he said "I suppose the British Consul sent you to me?" I replied that that was not the case and that we could expect little help from that source. This went down quite well, as I knew from Roger that the Consul was not at all liked in Ostend. However, he told us that he could not authorise free passages and he was sorry but he could not help. Thinking "In for a penny", and taking a deep breath, I said "Shall I ring Brussels?" He said, without a pause, "I will ring them for you". He rang a number, but the conversation being in Flemish went right over my head, apart from the occasional "Yah" or "Nein". When it was over and he had put the phone down I was on the point of leaving when he said, "They say you can go". What a relief. He added that we must be last on at Ostend and last off in Dover, and which ship did we want to go on?

I opted for the first ship next day, which gave us time to secure the KJ and inform England. He appeared to be almost as happy as I was that we could get fixed up. First call next morning was to Belgian Customs. I told them the story and asked whether they could inform the Special Branch Officer at Dover of the position. They agreed to do that and the officer I spoke to asked if I was one of the London police officers on board. Having replied "Yes" he said that we should get on board and keep out of the way.

The ship left at 1000; as it turned out, we were aboard *before* anybody else, although I had told them that we had been instructed to be last on and off; a Gallic shrug cleared that up.

We got into Dover about 1500 and were hanging about waiting for the gangway to be readied. Before anybody went ashore a three ringed Customs Officer came aboard and said; "Where's the Ostend Sea Cadet Party?" I said we were all present and said "Fall in here in two ranks". He went along counting and then said "Right turn, quick march" and off we went. I think this is what is meant by a friend at Court! Obviously the Special Branch officer at Dover had been told by his counterpart in Belgium what we had been up to.

A fortnight later a small crew went over, collected our most portable items (things such as binoculars, telescope etc., which we had left with Paulette) and brought the ship back, this time with no problem.

Since those long-away days Henri has died and Roger Albrecht has now retired from the sea, but we still keep in touch with him and Paulette.

Another eventful trip was the following year, 1966. We agreed on Ostend as a destination, but wanted to go a bit further. However, it was difficult finding somewhere not too far away with the chance of a reasonable berth. We had made Flushing (a port in the Netherlands, the Dutch name for which is Vlissingen) one year, but we had difficulty getting a mooring until we were eventually allocated one well away from the centre in an oil berth. It was difficult to get an idea from the chart as to the exact nature of a berth, although we did look at a place called Terneuzen, on the Maas. Eventually, having decided that we did not like the look of that very much as a destination, we decided on Flushing again, with Ostend as the first port of call.

On getting into Flushing John Cowan, the ex-policeman from Kennington, said that his wife had told him that her brother, who had been killed on a Merchant Navy ship right at the end of the war, was buried at Terneuzen. Apparently she wanted a photo of the grave and I asked him why on earth he hadn't told me this before. He felt that if it turned out to be pushing ourselves too far he would have felt bad about it. My view was that all we needed was a reason to go there, and now we had it. However, it was too late to sail, so after making enquiries about getting there by land we found that we could get a coach from the station, although they did not run very often. Eventually we decided to hire a taxi for the outward journey and work out the return later.

There were four of us in the party, three in uniform and one in civvies, John carrying a letter from the doctor in Terneuzen who had certified the death. We stopped at a café before going into the town but although the lady behind the bar did not speak much English, we showed her the letter nevertheless. Obviously she recognised the doctor's name so she went away and phoned him; in about 10 minutes he arrived by car and introduced himself. He told us to let our car go and he would take us in to the town to meet a friend of his who would help us as he had left a surgery full of patients and needed to rush back. When we thanked him he said something that we were to hear four times that day: "For an Englishman it is no trouble".

He took us to another café and introduced another Dutchman to us who was the Burgomaster; at home he would have been the local chief police officer. He told us that since the doctor had told him about us he had been trying to raise the sexton at the Church, but as he was out he had left a message for him to ring as soon as he came in.

It seemed that quite a lot of police business was carried out in the café , presumably to avoid any hardship! Once we had told him that three of us were police officers in London, and after one or two rounds of drinks, we were home and dry. We had a break for a conducted tour of the police station after which we returned to the café and took up where we had left off. And there it was again, when we apologised for keeping him from his duties: "For an Englishman, it is no trouble".

After about an hour and a half had passed, with no sign of the Sexton, the Burgomaster suggested that we went to the churchyard without him. Although he (the Burgomaster) did not know the exact grave, he did know that persons who had no known relatives were all buried in one small area. Although he was reluctant to say it, he obviously thought, as all the graves were exactly the same, did it really matter? Obviously we had to appear to agree, but fortunately on the way he saw the sexton on his bicycle, pedalling as hard as he could, with the church books in his carrier. He showed us the relevant entry in the book with the number of the grave and we soon located it. I took three photos of John standing there, with some flowers the sexton had produced from somewhere. I tried to give him a few guilders but he indignantly refused them: "For an Englishman ...."

Yes, he said it too.

By this time we were quite peckish, so we were pleased to find that, having returned to the café for a further libation, the Burgomaster's had told his wife of our presence and had taken a large plate of sandwiches to the police station. The fluid intake had been reasonably high and, up until then, we had had nothing to mop it up. Having retired to the station, not only did she fuss over us and more, but more people came in and wanted to shake our hands. We were British and, to them, we were the tops! Moreover, we were in the British Navy!

By about 10pm we began to think how we were going to get back. It then transpired that the last ferry had left but we could go to the other side of the island to a car ferry that ran all night. We didn't ask where it ran to, as we were in that pleasant state of euphoria where we didn't care if it snowed ink! Three of the friends we had made got their cars and took us to the ferry, which ran hourly. Needless to say our hosts insisted on giving us a good send off, and there just happened to be a café nearby. They had a little chat with the ferry ticket man after which we were escorted on board with almost tearful handshakes. We were then introduced to the Chief Officer of the ferry, whose English was probably better than ours! I asked him if he was English and he said he was not, but that he was Norwegian and had been in England during the war, serving in the Free Norwegian Navy; he was proud and pleased to be helping Englishmen.

Having told him we were bound for Flushing, he explained that there was no link on the other side. However, he could arrange to have us dropped at Middleburg, where we could get a train. He went down to the car deck and we were split into three cars, whose drivers said they would take us to Middleburg, although I am sure that their original plans did not have them going anywhere near there. But, of course, "For an Englishman ....."

We were all safely delivered in Middleburg at just about midnight and found that the next train did not leave for Flushing until 0120. That left us with an hour to wait and nothing open, with hunger upon us again. We looked in the café on the platform, where the chairs were all up on the tables and the staff were in the process of clearing up; obviously going home was their first priority. The manager saw us looking in and, having come to the door, immediately recognised us as English. His enquiry regarding whether or not he could help us was greeted with the answer that a few sandwiches would not go amiss, if that were at all possible. He had other ideas and, with the staff clearly as willing to help as he was, got the chairs off of a table, laid places and offered to cook anything that they had. We settled for steak, chips and beer, and although we paid for it, there was no question of them accepting a tip. They, too, were happy to do anything for Englishmen.

Having said our thanks, we boarded the ferry in a very subdued state, going over in our minds that we were British, English, and that to these people we were something special. For my part, and I expect it applied to us all, I was proud and humble to be the recipient of so much spontaneous good will. It was genuine, so pleasurable to us all, especially with so many people involved. It was, of course, still so very soon after the war and although we knew that we had carried the brunt of it for many years, these people knew it too; in whatever way possible, they wanted to say "Thank you".

Chapter 3 - The Kenya Jacaranda Becomes Ours

In the mid 1960s we lost our President and friend, but just before he died he rang me and said he had got somebody to put up a thousand pounds to buy the ship. He actually said "We'll change it into pound notes, put £800 of them on the table and she'll jump at it; then we'll put the change in the kitty". It didn't work out exactly like that, but nevertheless, in a very short space of time we found ourselves ship-owners.

With a prescience that we were later to bless, the ownership was vested not in the Unit, but in the name of the Commanding Officer and Chairman (Peter Harding and I). Being the owners at last we felt a renewed vigour to really start to work on her. The father of one of our Cadets was a shipwright and he gradually re-decked her, using softwood donated by the P.L.A. This solved our short term problem with the deck but in later years we were to rue the day we did it, but of course it is so easy to be wise in retrospect.

We were now working for 'our' ship and, as we got more and more involved in what we now know as DIY, we took more and more jobs on. This was not so much from choice but simply because we could not afford to have them done, even with all our friends in the docks and the local neighbourhood.

The Sea Cadet Corps, whilst happy to encourage us to take Cadets to sea and enhance the public image of the Corps, never ever gave us even the proverbial Widow's Mite. They did, however, pass on anything that came along that was of no use to the Navy that had come their way. A case in point that comes to mind was when a S.C.M. (Sea Cadet Memorandum) was issued inviting any unit who could use naval signal flags, or, as they called them, "Flags, Naval, Signalling for the Purpose Of", to indent for them. I was told by the Head of Stores, Len Archer, that I could have as many as I wanted, as long as I could collect them from the Naval Stores at Deptford. Len was then to be found in the corridors of Grand Buildings, Trafalgar Square and he was that most unusual of men, unique in the annals of the Royal Navy, a round peg in a round hole.

Having collected a sample of three or four I rang him at Sea Cadet H.Q. and asked whether he had seen them. He said that he had not and that they were a goodwill gesture from Plymouth Dockyard. I told him that they were certainly signalling flags, but for a Battleship or Aircraft Carrier; indeed, just one of them would cover the Jacaranda completely! His response was, "Well, use them for cleaning cloths, but remember that flags are consumable stores, (which meant that they could be "Used to Destruction") but the gun metal clips at top and bottom were permanent store items and would be on the Unit's Stores List". As at that time we had no Battleships and were a bit short on Aircraft Carriers it was obvious that Plymouth had a surplus of Flags, Naval, Signalling for ... and someone said "Let the dustman have them".

One other excellent example of Len Archer's workings was when two very large heavy crates arrived, out of the blue, at Stave Yard, Surrey Commercial Docks. They were marked "Bermondsey Sea Cadets - not to be used in any non-MOD owned vessel"(!), and inside were two Perkins P6 marine diesel 6 cylinder engines, each having a brass tag on it noting, "Serviced in 1942"

Never having any previous knowledge of these, I rang Mr Archer at the stores and to enquire what they were for. Very innocently he replied, "For instruction, what else?" When I asked what the "not for use in non-MOD vessels" markings meant as far as we were concerned, he said, "My dear Steve, you told me once that, in the police equivalent of QR & AI (Queen's Rules & Admiralty Instructions), there was a line that said, "Whilst rules cannot be made to cover every possible contingency, something must be left to the discretion of the individual officer". Of course!

We kept those engines for a long time and mounted an all out drive for funds. We held dances, jumble sales, sweepstakes, whist drives; collected waste paper, old iron, brass, lead, copper, car batteries, everything and anything that was capable of being sold. Eventually we had amassed enough to pay for the installation of our two 'new' engines.

However, they required something we had hitherto not had, a bank of batteries, and although we collected quite a few 12 volt car batteries, the engines required 24 volts. This meant an awful lot of batteries and at that early stage we were still very ignorant and did not realise that batteries were different and did not lend themselves to large and small being jumbled together. However, fate took a hand in our affairs yet again. A day or two after our first essay on battery collection, I took over the R/T car (a police Area Patrol Car) from the early driver and in the boot he showed me a large well-made mahogany box, complete with brass hinges and handles. It had a large broad arrow in several places on the outside and was stencilled on the lid "Batteries, Starting Tanks For, 24 volt". The driver told me that he had got it from "Enthoven's, down town; they're getting lorry loads of them delivered and they're chopping them up to get the lead out. Some are brand new".

This, frankly, I did not believe, but nevertheless we went hot foot - or rather hot tyre - to Enthoven's Ltd in Rotherhithe Street. It was a firm that I knew well, being manufacturers of anything made from lead. In their works lumps of lead were stacked up like bricks, only a bit bigger, with the weight painted on them usually, 25-4-2-11 which, translated, meant 25 tons and a bit.

Sure enough, when we got there a lorry load of batteries was in the process of being unloaded. Labourers were chopping up the beautiful mahogany boxes with axes and heaving the batteries to one side, where a fork lift truck was scooping them up and dropping them into a giant melting pot.

I looked at one or two of the cases and some of them had never been filled with acid; they were brand new. I asked one of the workmen who I should see to try to liberate one or two of them and was told: "Mr Harding's the Guv'nor".

Having been directed to his office I was confronted with what appeared to me to be rather a dour man who at first sight did not seem to be a good prospect for what I had in mind. Nevertheless, I explained to him about the K.J., where she was, the problems we had financing her, and how a pair of these batteries would be like manna from heaven. He did a little figuring on a notepad and said, "Each of these batteries means to me roughly 70 pounds of lead - I will give you a battery in exchange for every 70 pounds of lead you can get."

Although we had some scrap lead at the Unit it was not nearly enough, and the PC who was my wireless operator said, "What about Church or school roofs?" Though tempting, I didn't give that suggestion serious thought, but I did circulate a plea to everyone and anyone that old car batteries or lead in any shape or form would be most gratefully received at the Unit. I had left my 'phone number with Mr Harding and I very soon got a message asking me to drop in and see him some time, which I of course did. On entering his office he said (pointing to two obviously new boxed batteries), "These will be of some use to you. They are yours, and when they pack up I will change them for new ones".

I was not usually taken aback, but in this case I could hardly believe our luck. When I asked him how on earth new and obviously costly batteries such as these could be scrapped, he told me that there was an M.O.D. order that any batteries over a certain age held in stock must be scrapped, and these were subject to that order. The majority were brand new and he had selected two of those, filled them with acid and charged them. He told me a long time afterwards that he had gone to the Surrey Docks and asked the P.L.A. policeman on the gate where the ship was, if it existed at all. At that time he had obviously doubted my story but having been shown the K.J. in all her glory, by good fortune there was somebody working on her who told him that I was the C.O.

Having told him that, in my opinion he was wasted in his job and that he should be on our committee, to my surprise he said he would be pleased to come to the next meeting. He was as good as his word and has been on it until fairly recently and until age got the better of both of us, for many years he and I were President and Chairman respectively, and Trustees of the ship. His knowledge, business acumen and common sense have been at our disposal and, more than once, been invaluable.

As soon as the last training cruise was over we de-stored her of as much as was necessary and took her down to Messrs Cory's wharf at Woolwich, securing her to a floating pontoon. We had previously sent the two Perkins engines there by road and the firm had agreed to install them for us free of charge, only charging us for any parts they might have to supply.

As the deck over the engine room had to come up anyway we took the opportunity to make a hatchway so that, in future, when an engine had to come out we did not have to tear up the decking. Obviously, when they originally put in the Kelvins they must have dismantled them, put them below decks and re-assembled them down below.

We sent several working parties down to assist at weekends and the job got off to a good start. It took longer than it would have done in the ordinary way, as the firm had said that if they got a repair job in, that would have to take priority and ours would have to go on the slow burner.

This was fair enough, but we soon had another problem when the old propellers were taken off. They were unsuitable for the new engines, not only because they were right handed whereas the Kelvins were left handed but they would need to be a very different pitch. Again fortune favoured us; we found a firm in Mortlake who agreed to make us two new screws, to our specification, for £40 each. When they saw the old ones we were told that they should have been changed years ago, and that it was a wonder that they had not fallen to pieces. The manager of the firm demonstrated to us what he meant. He put a rod through one of the old ones and tapped it, the resultant sound being like a hammer hitting a piece of lead, yet when he did it again with a new propeller that one rang like a bell. This was the first, and by no means the last, time that we came into contact with electrolytic action.

When the time came to bring her back to the Surrey Docks with two engines that were approximately three times more powerful than the old ones, the result was very much an anti-climax; her speed was very much as before. The benefit to us was that they were much more reliable, but although we had much more power at our disposal we could use only a small part of it; to ensure that, we had a four-to-one reduction gear on each engine.

The pitch of the screws was altered and as far as we could see the only advantages were that we no longer had a hand start, we could dispense with the drip tray for knuckles and also get rid of what had been a veritable fire hazard in the 30 gallons of petrol slopping about in the deck tank. We left

Woolwich with a temporary diesel tank on deck, containing just enough to get us back. Then we had to rip out the petrol tank that had been let into the deck and thoroughly clean out the T.V.O. from the fuel tanks before we filled them with diesel. We also had a plentiful supply of electricity, albeit 24 volt, so we could have some lights! In due course of time we also acquired a radio and a fridge and later on an echo sounder.

Some time later we recruited an engineer who said, the first time he saw the ship on a hard, that we had the wrong pitch on the screws. I remember him picking up a nail from the mud, and saying "There's a formula for this, I can't remember how it goes, but perhaps we can work it out". We were by this time so impressed with our new engineer, Vic Meager, that working from his formula, we took one prop off at a time and had them recast in the new pitch. We could not do them together as we wished to have some control over the ship apart from sails. When they were both done we got another knot out of them and she handled a lot better.

Vic was an unassuming man, not very tall but a most unusual type, an engineer who knew the theory backwards as well as frontwards and could also put it into practice. As long as Vic was on board nobody worried if anything went wrong; whatever it was, Vic could, and did, repair it.

Work went on all the time. We bought a Douglas Fir tree (we unfortunately failed to get the Norwegian one from Trafalgar Square, but, although we got the blessing of Norway, we could not move the Ministry of Agriculture, who insisted that it was burnt!). From it we made a new mizzen mast, complete with boom gaff, crosstrees, yards and shrouds. It was 64ft long and tapered from 13" diameter at the base to 5" at the truck. We stepped it and set it up ourselves. Next we received an estimate for a new suit of sails from Jeykel's of £894, an impossible sum. It was DIY time again; we bought 30 bolts of target canvas, borrowed a heavy duty sewing machine from Edgington's the tent makers, and found a Mum who operated a similar machine. We took over Courage's garage at the rear of Tower Bridge Police Station, swept it, took the old sails there and marked them out on the floor. Relays of police colleagues worked the sails through the machine in two weekends and we took them back to the Unit where we did all the reef points, tabling, roping and cringles in by hand. Cost: £134.

Chapter 4 - The Bo'sun Arrives - and then the Mutiny

In the same year the death of the President was offset by the appearance of an elderly man who came on board one night just as we were closing down. The Quartermaster said that there was somebody who wanted to see the Skipper, so I told him to bring him aboard. He looked, at first sight, like an up to date Long John Silver, with a glass eye, an ancient monkey jacket, a pipe like Popeye's and three fingers missing on one hand. He was also, we later found out, diabetic.

He repeated everything two or three times, raising his voice by a complete octave each time. We found out that his wife was almost stone deaf and this was his normal routine. He said "My name's Mathews, Charlie Mathews. You've got a little lady here I'm very interested in, and I'd like to get to know her better".

My first reaction was that he was after one of the canteen girls as they were the only distaff element we had. However, he seemed too ingenuous for that, and when I asked him which particular one took his fancy, he said "Why, that little lady alongside, that there Kenya-something or other". A few minutes' conversation with him elicited the following: he had lost his eye taking a reef in the square rigger Iredale in 1904; he had been at sea since he was 14; been the master of a P.L.A. dredger, India, until he had to come ashore at the age of 65; and at the present moment he was night watchman at PLA head office on Tower Hill. In no time he was a fixture on the KJ, becoming the bo'sun; what he didn't know about sails and sailing was not worth knowing. All the gear that we had removed he put back, and a lot more besides. He taught us all a great deal, probably unknowingly, by the great depth of his own knowledge and expertise. After a while he brought a friend down, Bert, whose other name we never knew. He was a carpenter who worked very slowly and spoke very little, but anything he did was done to perfection; between the two of them they kept the ship on top line and it wasn't until they were not there that we realised just how much work they did.

We used to pay his fare to Brockley, where he lived with his wife on the fourth floor of a block of GLC flats. There were no walls, windows, drains or stairs in their flat; instead they had bulkheads, scuppers and scuttles, which neither of them thought in the least bit odd. Charlie had used this language for some 60 years and he knew none other. There were several sea cadet small boats where we were in the dock and one of their workers used to travel with our bo'sun on the underground to New Cross. Apparently the bo'sun nearly got him arrested one day when they had both been sitting in the train, waiting for it to start, when the bo'sun suddenly said, "I've had a lovely day today, I stripped the old girl naked. I got every stitch off her and stowed away, I've had a lovely day". When the train got to Surrey Docks there was a mass exodus from that compartment; however, the bo'sun never realised that he, having been misunderstood, was the cause!

Stories about him were rife as he was a larger than life character and there were very few ports he had not visited. At one stage he was employed on the gold mines in South Africa as a rigger and had to leave at a minute's notice one day when the manager saw he had a glass eye. Another day he was in the *wheel-house* with two Cadets on the wheel and I was amidships. Suddenly both lads came flying out of the *wheel-house*, alarm on their faces. I rushed along, thinking that perhaps age had suddenly caught up with him, but found that he was on the wheel, quite unperturbed. However, his glass eye was rolling round on top of the compass card; he had taken it out, put it there and said, "Keep your eye on that while I stoke me pipe!"

The years rolled by and we began to extend our area of operations, with Dover, Ostend, Flushing and Calais seeing us more and more frequently. Slowly, Sea Cadet H.Q. increased our paperwork for these trips until, to come in line with the Civil Service, we were obliged to submit an application for a foreign cruise in quintuplicate at least a month before each trip. One annual cruise to those four ports and home again had been applied for in the late 60s and been approved. The training Commander of the London area rang me at home one day and said "Your trip, old boy; I'm afraid it has been cancelled". As I had got approval I asked him why. He said there was a letter in the post to confirm it and that he was sorry but he could not tell me the reason. In vain I said this was the high spot of the year and if this was implemented it would knock the bottom out of the Unit. All he would say was "Sorry, old boy".

Having by this time managed to get contacts in many areas I asked around and found that the reason was that the Navy had got a purge on expenses and all cruises to the continent had been cancelled. Somebody pointed out that it would not be a good augury for the Navy if its only representative was a scruffy Brixham Trawler or an M.F.V., several of which had found their way to Sea Cadet units. That was the real reason.

We convened an emergency committee meeting where the whole thing was talked over. Finally the Chaplain, the rector of Rotherhithe, said, "I intend to form the St. Mary's Rotherhithe Youth Club. I am going to ask this committee to do duty as its committee, with Steve as its leader. I propose that membership of the Sea Cadet Unit implies membership of my Youth Club and I am going to ask this committee to lend me the *Kenya Jacaranda* for a nine day cruise to Calais, Ostend & Flushing. I would like that put in the minutes."

We could not find a flaw in this and when I told the Training Commander what we were going to do his only comment was, "Good luck to you old boy." When the day came we did a coastal cruise to Dover, where we spent the night, and brought in a new evolution. We lowered the Blue Ensign, removed our uniforms, changed into dungarees and singlets and hoisted the Red Ensign; then we went on the cruise. On the way back into Dover we reversed this procedure, and all appeared to be well – at least, until the newspapers got hold of it.

The particular time of year was called the silly season, when there wasn't much other news about, and anything out of the ordinary made the front page. The Daily Telegraph ran to two columns headed "A slight case of mutiny", the Express said "Turn your blind eye Nelson" and although I can't remember what the others said, they all had the story and my telephone ran hot. It seemed to me that the best plan was to give them all the exact story and let them make of it what they would. It was not a nine day wonder, not even a two day wonder, but the damage was done. I received a letter from

S.C.H.Q. citing the reports and asking me for my reasons, in writing, to account for the presence of the ship on the continent on the dates quoted. I said that the *Kenya Jacaranda* was not an Admiralty-owned vessel and that its presence on the continent was not disputed; she was there with a party of members of St. Mary's Rotherhithe Youth Club, of which I was the leader.

This did not suffice, and the Chairman and I were required to attend an official inquiry, at the Admiralty no less! Having duly attended, we were on one side of a long table, with the Admiralty flag at one end and the death of Nelson at the other, with little note pads and pencils aligned with mathematical precision by each place setting. On the other side was the Captain of the Corps, the Training Commander, a two ring Wren and the London Area Officer.

At the head of the table, resplendent in full uniform, was Admiral of the Fleet Sir Gilbert Stephenson, DSO, DSC etc., the Admiral of the Sea Cadets Corps, known during the War as the Terror of Tobermory. He was an autocrat in his own right. Stories about him and his works were legion, and woe betide and Commanding Officer who fell foul of him or did not come up to his high standards.

One story, quite true, was of an episode on board when the Admiral was due to carry out his first inspection. As he came to the top of the gangway he was piped aboard and greeted by a piping party and, as it was a cruiser, an armed party of Royal Marines. The Captain saluted, and as the guard came to the Present, the Admiral threw his uniform cap on deck and grabbed the arm of one of the piping party, shouting "That's a bomb!" The seaman, having been told that on this day anything could happen at any time, without further ado kicked it over the side where, with its burden of gold leaf, it straight away started to sink. The Admiral then shouted to the same seaman, "Man overboard," pointing to his cap, whereupon the seaman jumped into the sea and managed to recover it.

It was nothing for him to creep aboard in the middle watch (midnight to 0400) and, if he was not challenged, to take some article belonging to the ship back to his office. He would then make a signal to the ship requiring the

Captain to report to his office at 0800 next day, usually requiring him to bring the missing article with him. He was an Admiral who never grew up.

Anyway, back to the enquiry. Starting proceedings, he told the Wren Officer to read out (he nearly said "the charges") the file. She went into it from the original application, the granting of it and my receipt. She then went on to mention the presence of the ship on the continent and the Admiral said "So you disobeyed orders". When I replied "No Sir," he slammed his fist on the table and shouted it again. I said "The *Kenya Jacaranda* is not an Admiralty-owned vessel, Sir, she was there under the banner of the Rotherhithe Youth Club"; he shut me off and told me that he had heard of this so and so club and that it was a fiddle.

I agreed with him and he said, "We must have an undertaking that it will not happen again". I said "Give me your assurance that the need will not arise and I'm your man Sir". He said "Let's go and have a drink" and took me to the United Services Club where he regaled me with stories of punishments he had meted out to miscreants in his Service days. When he asked me where I had been I told him "All round the world and a bit". He asked "Africa?" and when asked where I told him "North, South, East & West". He told me that he had been a Midshipman at the battle of the Bight of Benin which made me duly impressed - I looked up the date of it later, but couldn't find it - it was probably before they started printing history books! We had an interesting day, but if the intention had been to overawe me it had failed dismally. In fact I told him while we were having a drink that he couldn't put me on half pay. When he asked why not, I told him "Half of nothing is nothing Sir"!

BRIXHAM TRAWLER TO THE RESCUE.—The Bideford-manned schooner Welcome, which was in distress seven miles south-west of the Wolf Lighthouse, being towed into Mount's Bay by the Brixham trawler Torbay Lass. The tow took 14 hours, being accomplished by sail alone.—Photo, Jenkin, Penzance.

An old photo from the archives of the Western Morning News.
It appeared on page 10 on Monday 20 May 1935.
[Photo courtesy of Plymouth Library Services]

Lady Claud Hamilton inspecting Bermondsey Sea Cadets

Dover and its white cliffs - June 1951

*Clockwise fromleft: Leading Seaman Moore, Leading Seaman
Poole and Chief Petty Officer Conroy*

Bermondsey Sea Cadets aboard the
Kenya Jacaranda at Boulogne in 1952

A grainy view of Kenya Jacaranda at
Bursledon on the Hamble c1951

Bermondsey Sea Cadets busy with the sails at Brixham

*Right to left - Lord and Lady Lady Claud Hamilton and
Captain R.J. Bowes-Lyon, MVO, RN at
TS Redriff, Bermondsey Sea Cadets base*

A pensive young Steve

Steve on board during her fateful refit at Maldon

The old and the new - Kenya Jacaranda and the Dome

Tower Bridge, Kenya Jacaranda and the Gherkin

Without the Gherkin

Kenya Jacaranda moored near a bar in Ostend

Kenya Jacaranda passing the National Maritime Museum

A grainy colour shot in Torbay approaching Brixham

The crew of Torbay Lass at work on the sails in the 1930s.
Left to right: 'Johnner Cole', first owner Alf Lovis,
an unknown crew member and Bill Parnall

Lady Genesta Claud Hamilton

The sun sets over the rigging

Steve Stevens where he liked it best - at the helm

A grainy shot from her days as Torbay Lass

The next three shots are of her 2001 refit at Lowestoft

Out of the water

Paul Ladyman in the wheelhouse

Sailing home

Looking up

Looking back

Just beautiful

Beached at Brixham in the 1930s

Chapter 5 - Cruising

Fund raising was ever to the fore in all our operations as there was always something we wanted, either as a replacement or simply an improvement and, to that end, we introduced into our weekend training cruises a "Recreational Training Cruise". We had to get clearance for this from our insurers, who were very reasonable; we explained that as the ship and committee had in its membership a very strong contingent of policemen it would be a good idea to have a complete crew of police officers one weekend, both as a training medium and also for fund raising purposes.

The first cruise started off quite well, arrangements having been made with Southend Police for us to both collect bait from the end of Southend Pier and to bring on board some local police officers. We had a full complement, most of whom had either been in the Navy or had some sea experience. We had plenty of food and made sure that we were not likely to run out of liquid refreshment. Just prior to berthing on the end of the pier I was informed that there was no water coming from the taps, to which I replied 'rubbish', but I was told there was none of that either. Anyway it turned out that the Cadets had been using the water in the dock and the tanks were empty.

I went ashore and saw the pier-master, a very harassed man, and asked if he could let us have a fresh water hose as we were right out. He said that he could not spare any time for us, and he was supposed to have a shore crew come to move a grand piano from the lower deck to the upper deck for a concert that afternoon. I told him that I had a piano moving party on board and that they could go to action stations at the touch of a button if he could provide us with water. He looked down at the ship, then the ensign, and said "They are a bonny lot of Sea Cadets". The piano was duly moved to his satisfaction and we had our water.

On a similar trip three months later, with a similar crew, we had fished in the Estuary and it blew up a little, so to get a comfortable night we decided to go into the Medway and anchor there for the night. This was before Sheerness Dockyard was closed, and just after we had anchored Garrison Point called us up by light and asked "What Ship?" We had an all round Morse signal light on each yard arm on the mizzen mast, with a key in the *wheel-house*, but it refused to work whatever I did. We later found that somebody had put 240 volts across it, and as it was 24 volt both lamps has fused. One of the Police crew had been a signalman in the navy and I said to him "See what you can do with a police torch, Nobby". Obviously it was hard going with an ordinary torch and he was busy for a long time, but he could see he was getting his message across as Garrison Point was giving him "T" after each word. When transmission both ways had ceased I asked him what he had sent. He told me that he had sent "*Kenya Jacaranda* manned by Metropolitan Police".

It must have struck the shore side as being a bit unorthodox, but as they did not come up again we turned in for the night, only to be awakened at 0200 by a bump alongside and a stentorian voice asking "What's the trouble?" I staggered on deck to find a Customs launch alongside with a full crew and a couple of policemen. I said there was no trouble that I knew of and we were just laying there for the night. The Customs Officer told us that they had received a message from Garrison Point, "*Kenya Jacaranda* anchored off here, boarded by Metropolitan Police". What could have been an international incident was only prevented by copious libations being offered and drunk and inter service relations going on into the smaller hours. How the question of a Customs launch with a full crew and police escort being sent about 20 miles from Gravesend was hushed up we never found out.

In 1964, just prior to my service with the police coming to an end, I was approached by a Police Inspector from the cadet training establishment at Hendon. He said that I would not remember him, but when he had been a sergeant at Lewisham he had been on one of our fishing weekends with the police. He suggested that, as venture training was the "in thing" for Police Cadets, how would I react to the suggestion of a weekend for them; they would do all the provisioning and cooking and make a donation to the Unit afterwards. I gave it some thought and then rang him, saying that I would agree but the trip but it would have to be made at a time when I was on duty; apart from that I could not see any problem.

We fixed a weekend date and after a trip to Hendon Police College and a chat with the Commandant, the cruise eventually took place. We had 12 Cadets, a Sergeant and an Inspector. The food was composed almost entirely of steaks which we cooked any way we liked, and there were always seconds; we had never eaten so well in our lives. After the trip, which went extremely well, I went to Hendon again for a post mortem. The Commandant was all for more and more cruises, but I said that the ship was first and foremost for Sea Cadet training and everything else took second place. It was tacitly agreed that perhaps one cruise a month could be arranged on the same lines as the first and a provisional date was agreed for the next cruise, some three weeks hence.

The paperwork was done at Hendon and some ten days later I was asked to ring the Inspector who had inaugurated things. Having done so he said; "Somehow the Deputy Assistant Commissioner has got hold of this and he has put a minute on it. I will read it to you - "An anomalous situation arises here. We have a PC in command of the vessel with Sergeants, Inspectors and possibly even higher ranks on board. What would the position be in an emergency? Furthermore, PC Stevens gives his time freely for the Sea Cadets, why can't he give it equally freely for the Police Cadets? Please report".

The Inspector asked for my reaction. I told him, "It is no thrill for me running up and down the Thames; I did so the last time as a goodwill gesture. The Job (what every police officer calls the Police Force) did not give me three 8 hour tours of duty, I gave *them* three tours of my own time of 16 hours each. For that weekend, I want three lots of 16 hours 'time off' and subsistence for the three days I spent away from my normal place of duty and out of the Metropolitan Police District. As far as any more trips with Police Cadets are concerned, forget it. Concerning the anomalous position, I have been away on cruises with three Chief Superintendents on board and nobody has ever given it a thought". He said "I was afraid that was what you would say, but I did not expect anything else". For the uninitiated, the Police did not *pay* for overtime, extra time spent on duty was repaid by entries on a 'time off' card, with the time owed taken off at a later date. I understand that things are much different now.

On Friday August 4 1967 we left London and anchored off Sheerness at 2200. Saturday August 5 was spent foraging at Sheerness. On Sunday August 6 we left at 0800 and anchored in Margate Roads at 016 Monday August 7; we later weighed anchor at 1025, entering Dover outer harbour at 1520. The weather deteriorated and we entered Wellington Dock on August 8. We left Dover next day, Wednesday 9 and sailed right through to 0935 on Thursday August 10, when we piped the side under sail at H.M.S. "Dolphin", Portsmouth. We moored alongside Sheer Jetty at 1020 and informed C in C (P) that we were on his doorstep. Commander Scott RN came on board in his official capacity as Area Officer, London, asked if there was anything we were needing, and having been told that we could use an extra 32lb Calor Gas Cylinder, he arranged for it to be brought aboard at 1355.

At 1820 The Captain of H.M.S. Devonshire came aboard, and having shown a great degree of interest he was shown over the KJ. The Cadets were all invited on board Devonshire for baths and a film show and, when they returned, piped down at 2300

Next morning we slipped and went alongside R.F.A. Robert Dundas for fuelling, topping up with 100 gallons of diesel and half a ton of water. We were told to move to No 1 basin entrance where we were entertained by the crew of H.M.S. "Dainty".

On Saturday August 12 we were give a new bake of bread from Dainty, but the Queen's Assistant Harbour Master (QAHM) told us to remain as there was a gale warning. On Sunday August 13 we all marched to Church Parade in the Dockyard Church; after Church Parade, at 1525, the gale had moderated and we slipped, piping H.M.S. Victory on the way out of the harbour. At 1955 we berthed alongside H.M.S. Warsash, the RNR H.Q. ship at Southampton. We informed Portsmouth where we were, their reply being "Gale warning imminent Force 8".

On Monday August 14 I went ashore with two Cadets and four holdalls containing 20 grey fronts which we wanted turned into white fronts. We took over a launderette, but of course Monday morning is wash day in any country, and the locals were not over-pleased to see three machines taken over by the Navy! We returned on board but the message awaiting us from AQHM Portsmouth was that the gale warning was still in operation.

Next day, Tuesday August 15, QAHM said "Gale Warning still in operation. Remain". At 1815 things seemed to be settling down and I rang QAHM. However, there was only a temporary lull in weather and we were told that we were not permitted to leave or to proceed West of Cowes.

We left at 1840, made Calshot Light vessel at 2200 and were in Cowes Roads and on a buoy by 2020. The log for the day shows, "Leading seaman Donovan falls in water from buoy. Picked up by motor boat. No damage to Donovan or buoy". Next day, Wednesday 16th August the first entry reads, "Hands to clean ship. L/seaman Donovan falls down on deck and sustains cut to hand. Sent to St Mary's Hospital". 1350 "L/seaman Donovan returns from Hospital, wound dressed". 1430 "L/seaman Donovan falls down companionway, sprains shoulder. Not Donovan's day." 2230 "Ropes doubled up, swell increasing. Gale warning still in force".

Wednesday August 16, "Remaining at Cowes, weather still unpredictable and too rough for us". 1755 "Weather forecast Humber Thames Dover Wight Gale Force winds".

Thursday August 17. Work of ship, leave given to both watches. 1355 forecast. No Change. 1755 forecast Westerly force 4-6 moderating. Viz poor.

Friday August 18 Weather, wind force 3-4 sea moderating. Message to C in C (P) *Kenya Jacaranda* proposes leaving for Portsmouth ETA 1700. Reply - Proceed.

Saturday August 19. All hands clean ship, misc. stores delivered for next trip, stored in *wheel-house*. 1410 Lt Commander Morin Scott arrives. 1430 Ship handed over for participation in Tall Ships Race as Sea Cadet entry.

Sunday August 20. In port.

Monday August 21. All hands employed in storing ship to 1500.. Slip and proceed to sea with launch in attendance for photographs. 1910 Off Ryde Pier, mainsail lowered and two reefs put in. More photographs, 2030 Photographer landed on Ryde Pier. 2150 Engines stopped and secured. Repairs to mainsail commenced (no mention of how it got damaged.)

Tuesday August 22. 0050 Course 200. Courses various to 0630. Bo'sun called to repair Mainsail. 1000 repairs completed. Mainsail hoisted. Various courses and sail drill. Wind light airs. 1900 Sails lowered, motorboat hoisted outboard and officer ashore to inform C in C (P) of position.

Wednesday August 23. 0001 Attempted to contact Tunbridge Wells by radio. Nil. Light airs continue, ship lost steerage way at 0600. 1800 Shambles light vessel, contact made by radio. No further entries in log for that day.

Thursday August 24. Attempt to contact Tunbridge Wells by radio, no joy. Light airs continue. Hands to sail and man overboard drill. 1700 Radio contact with Niton radio, passed to C in C (P). 2400 Numerous lights in sight.

Friday August 25. 0730 Sails lowered, hands to clean for entering Harbour. 0900 Enter Dartmouth Harbour. Secured to buoy at BRNC. 1255 Invitation sent to SRS Golden Hind. 1500 18 Sea Rangers aboard. Entertained. 1740 Shift ship to alongside RFA Pintail . 2040 Sea Rangers ashore. Main engines. 2105 harbour entrance. All sail. 2359 Course 090 (M)

Saturday August 26. 0630 Light airs. Ship barely making headway. 1450 Mainsail lowered to fit new throat stop. 1850 Man overboard exercise. Crew told that this was the last exercise, next time would be for real. 2355 Engines started to make Needles Channel.

Sunday August 27. 0250 Needles Channel. Enter harbour 1145, secured to buoy 1225. 1600 Stores embarked, crew to HMS Dolphin for baths. Secure 2300 Anchor watches set.

Monday August 28. Work of ship, prepare for sea. 1600 Slip. 1650 10 minute gun, 5 minute gun, engines stopped. 1700 Race started. Wind SW force 2-3. 2055 TV Camera crew alongside in launch. Wind SW b W, force 2-3.

Tuesday August 29. 0315 Wind Westerly force 2. 1100 Wind NW 3-4. Afternoon spent tacking against wind and tide towards Cherbourg. 2300 Close to Cherbourg entrance, wind failing and tide turning against.

Wednesday August 30. 0025 Ship not making headway. Anchor in 10 fathoms close to Cherbourg mole. 0530 Tide eased, sails hoisted, anchor weighed 0615 Enter harbour & cross finishing line. 0700 secured on trot in yacht harbour. 1145 presentation of prizes. (No mention of who got them, only of those who did not.) Anchor watch set.

Thursday August 31. 0700 Call hands. 0900 leave to 1200. 1310 leave Harbour. RMS Queen Mary leaving at same time! Wind SW force 4. Sail through night.

Friday September 1. 0005 Loom of Owers light seen bearing 339. 0400 Ship gybed. Topsail lowered to ease strain on topmast. 0900 throat & peak halyards both chafed. Sail lowered, ship rolling severely. Peak line carried away, gaff flogging and damaged radar reflector, jaws carried away. 1220 Wind SW force 4 2030. Entered Dover harbour, eastern entrance. Anchored in outer harbour. Anchor watches set 2240.

Saturday September 2. 0001 Violent rolling. 0800 All hands. 0910 CO ashore to get gaff jaws repaired. Customs on board. 1310 CO return with repaired jaws. Refitted. 1410 Weighed anchor. Violent sea encountered outside harbour. Follow buoyed channel to North Foreland. 2359 enter Thames.

Sunday September 3. 0340 anchored near Medway buoy. 0710 weighed, proceed up river all sail, negative top's'l. Max speed recorded on measured mile 9.6 knots. (With sail, engines and tide!) 1403 Enter Surrey Docks. 1530 finished with engines, ship returned to Bermondsey.

We were 'invited' to offer the ship to the London Area Sea Cadets so that they could put a ship in the tall Ships Race. We agreed to hand it over in Portsmouth on August 19, which we did, and got it back in the Surrey Docks after being away from August 4 to September 3. She was used as a National entrant vessel for 12 days. At no time did anybody from the Admiral of the Sea Cadets to the Ship's Cat ever say "Thank you" or anything approaching it.

Chapter 6 - Begging and Borrowing

The 70s came, and we were still working from Surrey Commercial Docks, but the nearest gate to the Unit, the North gate, had been closed; there was talk of the eventual closure of the whole Dock. I had left the Police, having concluded 30 years of exemplary service, and was working for the Greater London Council making [driving] licensing enquiries. Working from home gave me plenty of time for the ship now I had every weekend off, instead of, in the Police, only a full weekend every 8th week.

I had put the Bo'sun up for an award for meritorious service two years beforehand and he had been awarded the British Empire Medal; although there was no lower award he was very proud of it. Unfortunately he contracted cancer of the throat towards the end of 1970 and in the new year he was taken into King's College Hospital, where he rapidly became a pet of the nursing staff. The first time I visited him there I asked of him from the Ward Sister, her reply being, "Oh, he's a sweetie!" I told her that I had heard him called some things, but never that.

He didn't take kindly to hospital life, partly I think because he knew that it was terminal; the last time I spoke to him he caught hold of my hand and said; "I've only a hurricane lamp burning, Steve, and the last shackle's on the windlass". Almost "in extremis", he only knew his sea language; the next day he was dead.

One of the last episodes in his life that lives on in many minds was the day he had the bo'sun's chair on a lanyard rove off from the main topmast. He said to the smallest, and incidentally cheekiest, cadet, "Get in that chair, Son, I'll send you up aloft with a block and tackle. I want you to shackle it on to the eyebolt just abaft the hounds of the rigging". The kid looked at him with a blank face as he hadn't a clue what he was talking about, but Charlie said, "Go, get in it". The kid shrugged his shoulders and got in the chair, the bo'sun gave the order to haul him up, and away he went. The bo'sun called "High enough" and got his small telescope out that he always used for high up jobs. "Go on, get on with it".

The kid looked all round and when something about an eye bolt registered, he saw that he was stopped opposite one such. The other directions were pie in the sky as far as he was concerned, but he tentatively took the pin out of the shackle. He looked down at the bo'sun (who always had a short fuse when somebody failed to understand what was, to him, plain language). "Go on, get it in", he shouted. Galvanised into action the lad screwed the pin home and looked down. "Have you done it?" "Yes Bo'sun." "Right, lower away" he instructed, and the kid was very soon back on the deck bursting with pride. He'd done something right for the bo'sun, and very few people had ever done that. Bo'sun was examining the block halfway up the topmast and said, "You know what you've done, you've put it upside down".

The kid's eyes dropped and he looked at the bo'sun and hissed "You've got your bloody eye in upside down". Bo'sun was aghast, and looked at me for support. However, there was no way I could keep a straight face and I had to turn my back. In less time than it takes to tell, the bo'sun was chasing the kid round the deck, but with absolutely no hope of catching him. For a piece of impromptu Cockney wit I thought this one would take some beating.

On August 29 1971 the ship sailed from Southend with all hands dressed in Number Ones and at 12 noon, off Sea Reach Buoy No 2, engines were stopped and the sails let fly. The Blue Ensign came down to half mast and the Church pendant went up. Everybody was fallen in on deck and after a short committal service the ashes of Bo'sun Charles Mathews B.E.M. were scattered on the waters he had served not only for 17 years with us, but for many years before that. We knew that we would never see his like again and we were all very proud to have absorbed some of his vast store of knowledge and sea lore. It was the end of an era.

In 1973 the rumour of the closure of the Surrey Commercial Docks reared its head once again. We had on our committee the Harbour Master of the Dock, the Chief Police Officer and the General Manager of Harland and Wolff. Whether or not there was anything in the rumour, they were all treating it with a great deal of respect. The closing of the Surrey entrance, almost next door to the Unit, had been rumoured for years, but it still came as a surprise when the lock staff came on duty one morning, only to find another party from the contractor cutting the iron mooring bollards off with acetylene cutters and tossing them into the lock itself. It was done; signed and sealed as quickly as that. Whilst everybody realised that even if the dock closure did happen, it could not be done in that manner, it was obvious that the PLA, once committed, would pull out all the stops.

Over the years we had built up a small empire in the dock. We had bought a 25ft by 80ft shed from the Isle of Grain, erected a pair of heavy whaler davits on the quayside, put up a signal mast and halyards and laid 90 tons of concrete. We also had a 75ft semi underground air raid shelter that was full of gear that "might come in handy". Additionally, as a bit of window dressing we had a 12 pounder quick-firing gun weighing some 3 tons.

The Surrey Docks sailing regatta had become the biggest Sea Cadet function in the London Area. There used to be 80 races run in a day, with the KJ at one end and the motor launch at the other, connected with a borrowed telephone. Four standard pulling dinghies were at each end and, as soon as a race had started from one end, the next crew were ready to go off in the opposite direction. In this way we could, and did, get through a very heavy programme. Later on, when Units from Welsh Harp and Kingston areas elected to pull at Surrey Docks, we had to limit entries.

One of our ex-Cadets had a public house and he ran a beer tent; in addition we sold teas, sandwiches, buns and ice cream. The beer and tea tents were lent by Edgingtons, the tent makers nearby, and as is the case with times long gone we always seemed to have good weather. The PLA did not admit members of the public in any of their docks without a pass, for good reason. The only exception was the Surrey Docks Regatta, and it was a real family outing. There was plenty of grass to sit on and we usually put on a small show with the KJ, taking the young children for a run around the harbour.

It was 1974 when the blow finally fell; we were given notice to move all of our equipment and vessels out of the dock. We tried everywhere we could to find alternative accommodation, both for the Unit itself and also the ship. Eventually the PLA told us we could use an old social club in Lower Rd, Rotherhithe, within the dock boundary, as our headquarters. It was on the

53

understanding that, as the building was in an area that was scheduled for clearance, we would be expected to vacate it at short notice. However, we would not be charged while we were there; in other words we were semi-official squatters. This answered the problem of the H.Q., but it was a while before we found a berth for the motor launch and the KJ at Regent's Canal Dock, on the opposite side of the river. This belonged to British Waterways and we had to pay dock dues for the first time ever - I think it was £15 a month.

It was a very short hop across the river but, as we had a 112ft motor launch with no engines to tow alongside we had to be very careful as to how we went about it. There was no problem getting to the Greenland Lock, the exit to the dock, and we elected to get there just prior to slack water at high tide. Entrance to the Regent's Canal Dock could only be made for an hour either side of high water and the tide stands still in the river for about 40 minutes before it starts to ebb; we couldn't afford to be caught in the river when that happened, otherwise it would be first stop Tilbury. Fortune favours the brave, and we crossed the river at a time when there was no other traffic either way. We crept over to the north side and the lock keeper got the bridge swung and the lock gates open in time for us to go straight in. When we thought what could have happened it gave us the shakes.

It was a long time before we managed to get a shore supply of electricity. There was nothing laid on in the basin, but a tug firm gave us a long extension lead. This was essential for us, because we had electric bilge pumps in both ships, running off the KJ's batteries; the only way they could be kept charged without the engines running was to do it from a 240 volt supply.

Our tenure here was beset with pilfering, with any small items left on deck disappearing in no time at all. On several occasions the ML was broken into and appeals to the dock authorities were useless. There were only about three other vessels in the dock and we were told the only way to prevent trouble was to have a watch keeper, i.e. a full time ship-keeper. This was obviously not on, although we did inaugurate a system of flying visits, all to no avail.

Things came to a head after a three week period during which we lost a 10 man inflatable dingy, an outboard motor and, finally, the one thing we could never replace, the standard compass, complete with binnacle. This was unbolted from the deck and must have had a vehicle to take it away, but nobody saw a thing. The only other place we could hope to get a berth was St Katharine Docks, by the Tower of London. This had been the first of London's docks to be sold and it had been a success, with the old tea warehouses having been cleaned up and a new lock installed from the river on the Dutch pattern. For security there were patrols dressed up as 'Peelers', wearing frock coats and top hats.

To my complete surprise and gratification, the Dock Master, Ronald Phinn, was an ex PLA Dock Master. In answer to a letter telling him of our problems, he wrote saying that we were welcome to come in, and that we should get in touch with him personally to arrange an arrival time.

That we eventually did, and we duly installed ourselves there, having got the Navy to take back our ML as it had begun to show signs that it was nearing the end of its useful life. We were given a nice berth, with electricity and water laid on. At that time there were several historic vessels there; the old Tongue Light Vessel, that veteran of Antarctica *Discovery* and *Kathleen and May*, an ex trading barque. There were also several spritsail sailing barges and an ex London Fire float, Massey Shaw. There were also quite a number of other smaller, but nevertheless historic, ships, including a coal burner tug, a little coaster and a collier. The advent of an ex Brixham sailing trawler could only enhance the collection, especially as it was at no cost to the Harbour.

The only fly in the ointment was that there was nowhere to use as a store. As long as we had a foothold in the old Surrey Docks we could use that, but it was not ideal by any means as it was so far away. Also, there was nowhere we would be able to leave cars or indeed transport of any kind, when we were away for a trip. This was really a problem, as everybody had sleeping bags and kit to carry, not to mention all the food and drink required. However there was nothing else for it and we had to make the most of it.

One worthwhile event was the 150th anniversary of the opening of the dock. We were asked to take part in the celebrations, and in order to show her at her best we had to give the KJ a very quick short back and sides. We went out of the dock and lay on a barge for the run of the tide and then, at high water we had her dressed overall and approached the dock entrance. With 40 Sea Cadets in white tops and bell bottoms lining the side we led the procession of small boats in. She made a very good show, but to my sorrow we never managed to get a picture of her.

For some two years the log had shown on almost every trip, "Port engine stopped, or "Starboard engine stopped". The problem was usually the same thing, clutch trouble. The clutching arrangement seemed to involve about eight or ten large brass plates, which had to be taken out and shuffled, like a pack of cards, and then replaced. This is what it *seemed* to involve, but then I am no engineer! We tried to get replacements from the manufacturers and any ship chandlers, but nobody had any; this particular model had been discontinued years beforehand and there were no spares available anywhere. We had for some time been thinking about replacing both engines and had been saving money to that end. When we started making enquiries as to what we could afford and what would be the best engines for the money, nobody seemed at all interested in supplying them, at least not at the cost we had in mind. Eventually we compromised and settled for two Leyland diesels, which were identical to the standard taxicab engine, apart from marinisation. We got a reasonable discount, not from Leyland, but from the firm who did the conversion; the total cost was just under £4,000, including delivery.

Although there was nowhere we could have them delivered to at St Katharine Docks and no crane to do the lifting in and out, the dock manager of the West India Dock (which was due to be closed) proved most helpful. He gave us a berth at the head of the dock, next to the PLA canteen which was already closed; the road ran beside the berth. He said that we could have the engines sent to him and that he would store them until such time as we were about to install them. He stressed the point that we might have to move them at short notice, although he said that, in his estimation, the talking about closure could go on for a long time.

He was unable to (officially) help us with a crane, especially as we would be working at weekends. However, he would arrange for a mobile crane to be left outside his office, close to our berth, and leave the key in it. He knew that that Percy, our docker member, would know what to do with it; as long as it was back in situ by Monday morning he would be content.

We were able to use the old canteen for storage of some of the gear and the engines were duly delivered and appeared on the dockside, still crated. Our engineer, Vic Meager, said there was nothing to putting them in; as far as he was concerned it was just Meccano, but on a much larger scale.

In March 1975 we went to the West India and berthed very securely, with good long lines so that she was as close to the dock side as possible. There was hardly any rise and fall to contend with, and hardly any river traffic either. Using working parties was going to be the order of the day for a long time. The first task was to remove the port Perkins and put it on the quay. Our first thought had been that we could do the job in two halves, i.e. take an engine out and put the new one in, but this was vetoed by Vic; therefore, we turned the ship around and took out the starboard engine as well. Vic had armed himself with a small book full of figures and sums and he was very pleased to find that, with but a little alteration, we could use the same engine beds for the new engines. We, the labour force, cleaned out the accumulation of debris from the bilge and underside of the engine mountings, pumped it out and mopped it dry and gave it three coats of paint. She was so smart down there that I said it seemed a pity to put two grubby diesels in it!

All was set fair and the following weekend we got both new engines in and on their mountings; having done that we were able to get the decking back, caulked and payed. After that, Vic was down there at all kinds of times and in what seemed no time at all they were lined up and ready. The old engines were sold for scrap, but even then we got quite a fair price for them, money which did not go amiss.

For some time we had attracted interest from H.M.S. President, the London Division of the Royal Naval Reserve, and several members came down from time to time to help in all kinds of ways. On one particular Sunday, when we were still cleaning out the bilges, six members came down complete with overalls. One of them, a rather quiet man, was introduced to me as 'Pete'; he was told that I was the Captain (I must have looked the part after a couple of hours crawling about over oil stained boards). Pete said that he would do anything that was required - he was obviously not British, although his English was very good. I felt it would be hard to set him to work in the bilges, but he said that it was quite all right and down he went.

We had an arrangement, on the Sabbath, with a local Public House, the licensee of which had been one of our Cadets. I used to ring him in the middle of the morning and tell him how many bodies we had, and at 1300 or as near as possible, I would clean up and go to the pub. From there I would collect a gallon jar of pickled onions, two trays of beer and a steak and kidney pie each. On this particular day, having followed that routine, I got back alongside and unloaded. The first person I saw coming was Pete. I gave him a pie and a tin of beer and offered him the pickled onions; he took three or four. He seemed content and came back for a refill of beer.

When we were getting ready to go home the man who had introduced Pete said to me, "Do you know what Pete does?" Of course, nobody had told me that he was the Danish Naval Attaché to the Court of St James!!! The only thing I could think of saying was, "I'll bet it will be a long time before he gets lunch served that way again". I got the impression that Pete's day with the RNR would be included in after dinner speeches for many years to come!

The fitting out, testing and final tightening down of the new engines took some time, which was now of the essence, and by the time the boating season came we were eager to give them a full trial on the river, rather than merely steaming up and down the dock.

On July 18 1975 we did a usual weekend trip, went alongside Southend Pier and on to Gillingham where we topped up with diesel fuel. We also managed to exchange five of our old batteries, which we used for augmenting the power supply for all the extras. Nothing untoward happened and we resolved to give the new engines a really good run.

On Friday August 22 1975 we got away to a good start and anchored for the run of the tide off Southend at 2055. The anchor was weighed at 0200 on August 23 and at 1930 we were in the Commercial Dock in Ostend. We renewed our friendship with the Albrecht family, spent Sunday and Monday in Ostend and left there at 0615 bound for Calais, where we berthed at 1430 Tuesday August 26.

On some of the previous trips to Calais we had great difficulty in making contact with Portsmouth to inform them of our movements and had made our number known to the British Vice Consul, Mr Evans. He had agreed to inform Portsmouth or Chatham of our intentions when we either called on him or rang him.

When we rang him he told us that there was a collection of Naval ships from Germany, France, Holland & Belgium in port. There was no representative of the Royal Navy there and he asked if we would be at the Yacht Club and meet the others as the British Navy. I could imagine the reaction of the *proper* Navy at home, and wondered what they would say if they found out, but decided that I would cross that bridge when we came to it, or it to us. Mr Evans said that he would like to visit the ship, possibly with one or two friends; would 1000 on the following day be all right?

As soon as we knew we put all hands to cleaning stations. We had stopped wearing uniform Number Ones some time previously and most of us wore battle dress. I had a pair of the [Police] Commissioner's flannels, i.e. uniform trousers, and I did the best I could to clean them with petrol. One of the other policemen had his Number Ones with him and made a great play regarding being the only one in proper rig. When, however, he realised that he did not have the uniform trousers the laugh was on him. I suggested that he could deputise as cook and wear an apron.

Promptly at 1000 the next day, Wednesday August 27, Mr Evans arrived and was piped aboard. Fortunately all the lads had their uniforms and we had certainly cleaned the ship up, but we knew of old that making a silk purse from a sow's ear was just not on. Mr Evans brought one friend with him and introduced us. His name was Mr English and he was the manager of

Townsend Thoresen Ferries - he said that we could always call on him if we were in a jam. I told him of our earlier experience with the Belgian Marine and he told me that we had probably been returned to the U.K. as D.B.S. - Distressed British Seamen.

I think Mr Evans was very aware of our predicament and the inspection went well. He contented himself with looking around the upper deck, and then had a talk with the assembled lads and crew. We went afterwards to the Yacht Club and, I hope, did not disgrace ourselves.

Next day we slipped at 0300 and ran right through to Tilbury Landing Stage where we cleared Customs at 2010. The Port Authority agreed to us staying there overnight and we informed Chatham. Next morning at 0600 there was thick fog and therefore no question of leaving while that lasted. Eventually, by 1300 it had cleared and we left Tilbury, docking in St Katharine Docks at 1830.

In 1977 we resolved that we would be present at the Royal Review of the Fleet by Her Majesty the Queen. That was to be our first trip of the year, so up to June we really gave the old girl the biggest clean up ever. We left Regent's Canal on June 22 with a mixed crew of Cadets from Bermondsey, Woolwich, Dulwich, Greenwich and Southwark. Leaving on Wednesday we were giving ourselves plenty of time, especially as we were low on fuel and wanted to visit Chatham on the way in order to put that right.

We berthed at Gillingham Pier on Thursday June 23 at 0135, after an uneventful night run and took 350 gallons of diesel and a ton of fresh water. I also renewed our friendship with the submarine base in the dockyard and changed 8 batteries.

We left there at 1640 and another night run brought us outside Dover Harbour at four minutes to midnight. We only had to wait a very short time before being told that we could enter the outer harbour, which was very much appreciated because waiting anywhere outside of Dover means a lot of rolling. We entered at 0030 and anchored in the harbour, but did not go into the inner harbour. We left again at 0745 on June 24, reaching Newhaven at

1830 where we were allowed to berth alongside a dredger. We informed Chatham that we would be leaving for Portsmouth at 0800 on June 25.

Leaving on schedule, we had a soldier's wind (wind abaft the beam, ideal for sailing) along the coast. We lowered the sails at 18.05 and reported to C in C's office by radio, requesting berthing instructions. After a pause we were asked to give the name of the ship again. We did so and after a further pause we were asked, "What nationality are you?" I was sorely tempted to reply "Swiss" or "Hottentot", but discretion won the day. However, I did tell them that we had been reporting by radio for the previous thirty six hours. Such is fame.

We berthed alongside H.M.S. Rame Head at Whale Island, where we managed to top up with fuel again.

Sunday June 26 was used for a final spit and polish and the next day, Monday June 27, we left harbour at 0800 and sailed past the Sea Cadet flagship T.S. Royalist. She was in company with some seven or eight miscellaneous Sea Cadet ships on a rehearsal of the review. By this time the review had been altered, to take place 24 hours later on account of the weather. Just for the hell of it we saluted the captain of the Corps on Royalist by cheering from the side and waving our caps; possibly on account of this we were adjudged runner up for the smartest vessel award.

At 1400 the Royal Yacht went past the line of motley craft and Her Majesty was duly saluted. It was a great pity that the weather was so inclement and it was little short of a miracle that there was not a single hitch.

Everybody seemed to be left to their own devices. We asked the signal tower for berthing instructions but were told that they could not help and that we would have to do the best we could. We berthed alongside Rame Head again, but were told that we couldn't stay there; try Clarence Yard. They couldn't have us and we began to think that we were going to be the Flying Dutchman of Portsmouth Harbour.

We went back to Rame Head and found a nice berth on the opposite side of the harbour from which I thought nobody was going to get us away. I was proved very wrong in about 15 minutes, when a Dockyard Police vessel came alongside and told us that we were in The Royal Yacht Britannia's Berth; we went away again until we found a little slot in 'G' yard, that nobody else knew of, where we were finally left in peace. We left for home on Wednesday June 29, having to escort T.S. Barham for our pains back to London.

It was not until I left the Metropolitan Police, in 1966, that we realised the vast amount of help they had afforded us over the years. The Superintendent at Tower Bridge, one of many ex-colleagues with whom I kept in touch for a long time, told me, in confidence, that the 'phone bill at Tower Bridge dropped by over 10% when I left! He also said that the monthly mileage of the Station Van had also shown a considerable decrease. There were many occasions when I could have been called severely to account – once, perhaps, if the early turn Duty Officer at Rotherhithe Station had seen us before we saw him one summer Sunday morning at 4.30am, when a Police area car was crossing from one dock to another with a 1 ton concrete mixer in tow. We learnt afterwards he was bemoaning the fact that West Ham had lost the previous day.

On one occasion I was trying to get hold of some 2" FSWR (for the uninitiated, Flexible Steel Wire Rope, normally used for cargo winches on cargo ships). I was told that the stevedore foreman in Cunard's shed always had a few lengths of 2nd hand FSWR spare, so I duly approached him one day when I was driving Mike 6, the local area car. To the question, "Have you got a few fathoms of second hand 2" FSWR", he replied to the effect that he "Hadn't got any so-and-so second hand FSWR" and turned away. Just as I was on the point of giving him what Mr Churchill had made his personal sign he said "What's wrong with new FSWR?" I said, "Nothing at all, but I only want to moor up a sea cadet ship". To this he replied, "How was I going to get it out of the dock?", I replied, "You supply it and I'll worry about getting it out". Within a couple of minutes a 120 fathom length of new 2" FSWR, wrapped in oiled sacking, was on top of the radio in the boot and we were in business.

One day we almost arrested a short, very red-faced man we saw coming from behind a line of parked lorries in a side street in Bermondsey. At the other end two little girls had also come out , and all three of the car crew had the same thought, especially as the man got on a cycle and started to pedal away. I shot out of the car and ran after him; although we were all in plain clothes, everybody in the area knew what we were and most of them had the same idea about our parentage. I called to him to stop, but he just looked around and stood on the pedals, so I got hold of him and said we wanted a few words.

His reply was a request to take my so and so hands off him, and matters started to get a little heated, even more so when he realised what we suspected. The PC who had been our observer, who had a short fuse anyway, did little to help by telling the man to keep his trap shut; by the time we realised that nothing untoward had taken place and the two girls had been placated it was too late. The man we had stopped was a man who would do anything for kids and there was no way he would accept our apologies. In the end the Superintendent went to his address and smoothed him over, by which time the man went as far as to say "I suppose they were only doing their bl**dy job".

A week or two afterwards I was watching the driver of a Ford lorry, one of a fleet of such vehicles, moving garden produce from market to shop. He was sheeting the load over and I asked him what was the size of the tarpaulin sheet. He said it was 8 x 10 feet. I asked him whether his firm would lend me one for a weekend, explaining that I ran a local Sea Cadet Unit and that we had a crew going away for a week on our sailing ship and we wanted to make an awning over the foc'sle. He said, "Go and see Joe in the yard, tell him its for a boat and he will give you one". I asked him what Joe's name was and he said, "Everybody knows Joe, he ain't got another name".

Arriving at the firm of Thomas, Potter Priestly in Jamaica Rd and crossing from the pavement to what appeared to be the office, I was met by our red-haired friend of the cycle episode. He stopped short and asked me what I wanted. Telling him that I want to speak to Joe, he asked what I wanted him for. That could only be answered by, "You tell me where I can find Joe and

I'll tell him. Needless to say, he *was* Joe.   I had begun to have a hollow feeling that this was going to be one of those days, so I said "I'm sorry, it doesn't matter" and started to walk out of the yard.

His curiosity was by now aroused and he fell into step with me, asking "What's it all about then? You didn't come here to ask my name, you [so and so] know it".   I told him that it didn't matter, that I just wanted to ask you about a boat for some kids. He said, "A boat. Kids. Come in here".   I went into his inner sanctum and had a job to get out in under an hour; I went away with a tarpaulin sheet, a coil of rope, some paint, a bunch of bananas and a friend for life.

It turned out that Joe would do anything for anybody and was a soft touch for any local hard luck story. He was on board one day as engineer along with our chaplain, the Rector of Rotherhithe.   Although Joe rarely swore, he could never be accused of being couth. However, when the Rector asked me who he was I told him, "Believe it or not, he is a Christian and they are a bit thin on the ground around here".

Joe had two sons, one of whom was also called Joe; they were Big Joe and Little Joe. One year we had a shock call from the PLA that the ship was full of water and they had to bring in a tug to pump her out. This was in February, following a very hard winter; one of the sea cocks had frozen and cracked. When the thaw came, with nobody in attendance she had taken enough water to completely cover both engines, which meant, of course, that they both would have to be stripped right down and rebuilt, with all of this having to be done in our spare time. There was no way that we could afford to pay anybody to do the job. However, Big Joe heard about it and came down, along with our own engineer, George. He said that he could manage to do one, but only one, in the time available. Having heard that, Joe said, "Let George do one and me and Little Joe will do the other one". And they did.

My police and cadet relationship was not all a one sided affair; I was a good copper and the Police got their money's worth from me. At one time we had as Commissioner a very far sighted man, Sir Robert Mark. His creed was that, if any policeman was helping with a youth club and keeping youngsters off the streets for two or three evenings a week by so doing, he was obeying the initial precepts of the Metropolitan Police. These, laid down in 1839, stated that the primary object of an efficient police was the prevention of crime. He made an order that any police officer so engaged could be deemed to be on duty.

Shortly after I left the Police a Collator was officially appointed at every station. His function was to garner every item of local information and to file and cross reference it. Particulars of local villains, their habitat, friends and modus operandi were high on the list and eventually the Collator's office became one of the most useful places in any nick, - sorry, Police station. (Of course, Collators are long gone now – they have been replaced by Divisional Information Units.)

In the latter half of my police career, with sons, and even in one or two cases, grandsons of ex-Cadets in the Unit, I was a mine of local information. In most cases I knew their parents, their parent's jobs, how many pups the dog had and who put their sisters in trouble; how many previous convictions their uncles had and whether mum and dad were wed or not. On one occasion we pulled up a suspect van driven by a likely looking lad. For starters I asked him what his name was and he said, "You b--well know, don't you? Sir!" My colleague asked me later how come one of the local tearaways called me Sir. Another time I was waiting for a tram opposite Tower Bridge Station where, opposite, a young couple with a push chair were starting to carry it up the steps to the front door. The man, a typical Bermondsey son, looked sideways, muttered something about B coppers to his lady, then his face broke into a broad smile and he said pointing to the child. "Hello sir, can I put his name down for the Cadets?"

Many of these ex-Cadets and their sons work on and around the river. Several of them are part of the crew of the many pleasure steamers that ply up and down the river and, on the odd occasion when the KJ goes up-river instead of down, it is seldom that we do not get a whistle and a salute from one of them, which is heartening to say the least.

Chapter 7 - Goodbye to the Sea Cadets

The last cruise undertaken with Sea Cadets was a ten day one to France, Belgium and Holland and it was beset by trouble from the word go. Slipping at the start from Tower Bridge at 0400, both engines suddenly stopped and we ran into a trot of barges, fortunately with no more damage than scrapes and a loss of paint and dignity. Gale and near gale force winds regaled us for most of the time and we broke the main boom on the way to Flushing from Ostend; this was repaired temporarily by the Royal Dutch Navy. We had a fire in the engine room, which we were able to deal with ourselves, and on the last leg a NATO exercise in Ostend was abandoned and all hovercraft sailings cancelled on account of the bad weather.

In the interest of safety we sent the Cadets back to Dover on the mail boat on the morning of Sunday 20th July 1980. In the afternoon the weather had moderated somewhat and we decided to take the KJ home. At 1735 we were almost within sight of home when, off the North Foreland, a heavy squall struck and blew out the foresail; at the same time the starboard engine stopped. We rove off the jib as a staysail, but this parted; the anchor would not hold and it was a toss up which we hit first, Margate Sand or North Goodwin. Margate lifeboat came out but could not hold us and she got her warp foul of our port screw, which left us without power of any kind; we ended up in Ramsgate on the end of a tug's towing line with a lot of damage.

Once we had reached safety and informed the authority, messages came thick and fast from all and sundry. As we had no R/T the Harbour Master, none other than Ronny Phinn, one time Harbourmaster at St Katharine Docks, had to send somebody to us. In the end I made a transcript of the whole trip from Ostend from the log and had half a dozen copies made.

EXTRACT FROM LOG OF "*KENYA JACARANDA*" 18-20 July 1980

18 July

0020   On passage from Flushing to Ostend. Shipping forecast. Gale warnings Humber, Thames, Dover,

	Wights, Portland. SW to W force 6 increasing gale force 8 later. Viz Mod
08:00	C.O. to Belgian Naval base, Ostend. Gale warning still in operation. To Duty Staff Officer, Chatham, "Remaining Ostend and telephoning later". Wife of C.O. informed re notification of N.O.K.
13:08	Gale warning still in operation, no moderation in sight.

19 July

0730	Weather, West Hinder L/V. WSW force 7, veering Westerley. Harbour entrance SW force 5.
0900	C.O. to Belgian Naval Base. Forecast Dover. SW 5-6, occasionally 7 or gale 8, veering W 5-6 Rain. Viz mod, Outlook moderating to NW. To D.S.O. Chatham; "leaving Ostend 1300 for Thames"
1125	Locked in
1145	Locked out.
1200	Pierhead.
1217	Binnenstroombank Buoy. heavy rolling. Fore and mizzen.
1225	Gusting force 7 Foresail ripped. A/C 180'
1235	Entrance. Lower mizzen.
1410	Weather forecast. Dover Thames. SW veering NW 6-8, fog, rain.
1440	C.O. Ashore, message to DSO Chatham. "K.J. returned re adverse conditions". Enquiries at Consulate re return of Cadets to U.K. No joy at P & O Jetfoil base, all sailings cancelled. Final arrangements made for party of 10 to Dover by Sealink at 10.05 20th July. Message to C.O. Hornchurch Unit requesting transport arrangements at Dover, agreed. C.O. Ilford Unit informed, Cadets told to pack.

20 July

0700	Lt Waltsleben CPO Lawrence, Mr Davis, Cadets Ayres, Chittock, Wilson, Hardiman, Stanley, Darley & Daubney discharged to shore.
1050	Message to DSO Chatham; "K.J. sent Cadets home on 10.05 mailboat. Adult crew taking vessel home to London, leaving 1100". Reply; "Have a good trip". Forecast Thames, Dover. SW 6-7, occasionally 8 veering NW 6 later. Rain, Viz mod. State of sea at West Hinder L/V SW force 2
1103	Harbour entrance
1113	Binnestrombank buoy
1156	Oostendebank West. Wind N force 4.
1445	Set flying jib and mizzen.
1600	Falls L/V, Port bow
1644	Falls L/V abeam. Wind WNW 6.
1735	Jib halliards parted. Sail secured on deck.
1758	N. Goodwin L/V abeam to port 6 miles.
1910	Stbd. engine stopped. Jib rove on foresail halliards. Heavy rolling, mizzen bracket broken.
2005	V. heavy rolling and pitching. Vessel not answering helm. PAN call to N. Foreland, referred to Margate Coastguard informing them of position. Reply, suggest berth available at Ramsgate. Reply; "We cannot make Ramsgate, ship not answering helm. Do you wish to declare emergency?"
2015	Yes - Margate lifeboat on way
2045	Kent Police launch on scene.
2050	Lifeboat alongside. Tow taken.
2055	Tow parted
2102	Tow retaken
2110	Tow parted
2114	Tow retaken. Lifeboat sheers off. about 8ft on Prt gunwale ripped out.
2125	Port engine stopped. Tow from lifeboat round port screw.
2140	Tow parted. Tug from Ramsgate on R/T.
2143	Tow retaken

2148	Lifeboat unable to hold vessel. Anchor dropped in 6 fathoms. Still dragging. Tug Lorna B on R/T from Ramsgate. "Do you wish for assistance? We can only provide it on you signing Lloyd's open charter."
2155	I appear to have no choice
2230	Tug on scene
2241	Tow passed, prepare to weigh.
2256	Anchor cable jammed in hawse. In trying to free it. Lt Woodhouse injured right hand. Emergency dressing applied.
2355	Anchor cable cut, buoyed and slipped.

21 July

0005	On tow to Ramsgate
0020	Tug anchored off Ramsgate. Cannot enter because of low water.
0030	Lt Woodhouse taken off by lifeboat to Canterbury Hospital.
0115	Weather. Wind NW force 8 Storm cones hoisted 3 hours previously. R/T Watch set with tug. Both gunwales rolling under and V. heavy pitching.
0115	Conditions still the same
0200	" " " "
0300	" " " "
0400	" " " "
0500	" " " "
0541	Tug shortens in.
0545	Aweigh
0610	Tug Helena astern
0620	Ramsgate entrance
0625	Enter harbour
0630	Lorna B casts off.
0650	Berthed alongside
0730	C.O. Ashore. Message to DSO Chatham: "KJ berthed Ramsgate on tow after engine failure and loss of sail in

Thames estuary on passage from Ostend. Margate lifeboat called out. Full details to follow. Enquiries re Lt Woodhouse. Ten stitches in finger of right hand, discharged 0300"

0915	Customs and immigration clearance.
0930	Message from Margate SCC Engineer on way at 1000
1030	PO from Margate Unit with offer of help.
1200	Mr Winter discharged to shore. Message via HM "Ring Cdr Gay"
1300	Message via H.M. "Ring SOO Chatham"
1500	Lt Townsend, Ramsgate Unit aboard with practical offer of help. H.M. going to move vessel to outer wall at 1600. Mr Lawrence discharged to shore.
1630	Message via H.M. "Ring Mr Kemp at S.C.H.Q.". Vessel not moved. Work on clearing up. Drying sails, pillows, bedding and lifejackets and pumping out. Lt Acaster, ex Bermondsey, now Margate SCC aboard.
2130	C.O. & Lt Acaster ashore.
2300	Turn in, first time since 19th.

I remained with the ship for a week, as she was making water all the time, but it gradually lessened. One thing we did bless and appreciate was the R/T, which had enabled us to be on an R/T net with the Coastguard, Kent Police boat, the tug and the lifeboat; it really earned its money then.

After some four weeks in Ramsgate we managed to effect temporary repairs and got her back to London. The actual damage was dealt with under insurance, but the strains she had undergone brought forward many latent defects which finally brought home to us that merely making do would no longer suffice. A provisional estimate was made of £50,000, but in the event it was an under-estimate by 100%.

At this stage the Sea Cadet Council and the M.O.D. opted out, saying that there was no place in the training programme for the ship. (That was the first time I knew there *was* a training programme.) My commission was terminated and all naval stores had to be returned forthwith; this in spite of her, and our, record. We had, over the period 1951 to 1980, taken over 3,000 Sea Cadet personnel to sea under sail and had spent a total of 851 days at sea, all of which was, of course, voluntarily.

Chapter 8 - the MSTS is born

Thus the Mayflower Sail Training Society was set up with a capital of £10. It was formed from members of the PLA and Metropolitan Police (I had retired long since from the Police), H.M.S. President, ex Sea Cadets, the Royal Naval Reserve and some three members of the old Sea Cadet Unit Committee. The object of the Society was to continue to run the ship as before but, with the loss of the greater part of our old friends, fund raising now became my main object in life.

Before we had realised the full extent of the repairs we were faced with, we made an application to the London Dock Development Corporation for a grant towards a new deck. We had begun to think that this application had (with all other requests for help) died the death when, out of the blue, it was confirmed that they had awarded us £15,000. Coming, as it did, when our hopes were at a very low ebb, this gave us a great fillip; we started looking round for a ship repairers in the lower reaches with the necessary expertise with wooden ships, but they were few and far between.

On the point of foreclosing with a firm at Gravesend for a steel deck, we were approached by the manager of a ship repairers from Maldon in Essex. He had been told of our problem by a member of our Society. He offered to give us an estimate for the fitting of a traditional wooden deck. This was clearly a much more attractive proposition than a steel deck, and given that it seemed to be an ideal solution to our problem, we agreed to ask for an estimate. Unfortunately, he had been told the amount of the grant by our Member; not surprisingly, the amount of the estimate coincided with that of the grant almost to the penny! Obviously we should have kept the amount of the grant to ourselves and, had we done so, we could well have had a very different result. How easy it is to be wise after the event; how often, over the ensuing years, were we to have it brought home to us!

The KJ went to Maldon on 30 January 1983 and before we went any further we sought a complete survey from the most used surveyor thereabouts. This was done between April and June 1983. I had applied to the GLC some time previously for a grant towards a complete refit, but with the imminent demise of that body we had been told that we had missed the boat! However, just when we were beginning to think that we were going into the firewood business in a big way, we were told that our application had been put back into the system. We never knew the why, but of course we were overjoyed that a lifeline had been offered to us.

The total estimate was for the complete restoration of the ship was £70,700. This was submitted to the GLC, who added a 10% contingency and a further sum for the surveyor, which gave a rounded up figure of £88,000. We were told that there was no reason why this should not be approved at the next meeting in December. The whole project HAD TO be completed before their demise so we were told that we could, unofficially, start work if we were so inclined. The proviso was that if for some reason the grant was not agreed, the onus was on us. This was probably on account of the shortage of time and as a help to us - we instructed the shipyard to start work straight away.

Suffice it to say, and to cut a *very very* long story short, the KJ went to Maldon in January 1983 and left on 26 April 1986. The work had NOT been done, or at least had either not been done at all or had not been done to our satisfaction. It precipitated a very long and bitter dispute, going as far as the High Court, and it left us virtually destitute.

On the weekend of August 9 and 10 1986, after three months of weekend working parties to complete the work that should have been done at Maldon, we took the ship out into the river and ran down to Tilbury buoy just to loosen her up. Rounding up at Shornmead we retraced our passage up river. Broadness, Crayford Ness, Dagenham, Margaret Ness. We had to get clearance for the Thames Barrier, then Greenwich and Wapping. At Tower Bridge we rounded up and took 670 litres of diesel fuel from the fuelling barge, which we had to pay - that was a precedent, the first time we had *purchased* diesel, and it hurt!

Outward bound again -we reached Deptford, which was the last bit of the river that had a Royal Navy presence. It used to be Royal Victoria Yard and was, up until the last war, the victualling yard where the rum for the Navy was landed from the West Indies. It came in here as unbroken spirit, or in other words neat rum, and was then mixed with water and sent to ships all over the world. In the blitz of London's Docks in 1940, the Germans dropped incendiary and high explosive bombs and set alight all the docks on the south bank. Dockers, policemen, firemen and anybody in range were all affected by the fumes from the burning spirit; they were all reeling about drunk without a spot of liquor having passed their lips. People as far away as Lewisham were affected by it and the buzz went round that Hitler was using gas filled bombs; several people were reported to have asked for more!

The old Naval yards had been taken over by a company called Convoy's, who dealt in newsprint. Their big low loaders, loaded with massive rolls of paper weighing several tons, used to go from Deptford, via the Old Kent Road, over the river to the newspaper-land that was Fleet Street to be used for the next day's newspapers.

Several of the drivers were ex Bermondsey Sea Cadets and Convoys were well disposed to us; they had allowed us to put two ex-Admiralty railway wagons that we used for storage in their yard. We had been given them by Chatham Dockyard and without them we would have had a lot to trouble finding alternative storage space. We had imagined that we would have had this facility for as long as we needed it, but with the imminent closure of the yard we were out. It should have been obvious to us that this was in the wind, as two of the big newspaper groups had already vacated Fleet Street and set up anew in the new development that had previously been the West India, London and Millwall Docks. Here they would not have to cope with moving their paper in penny numbers and could stockpile it as they wished. In fact Fleet Street became closed completely as far as newsprint was concerned, in under three months.

We had managed to get a small section of one of the large cargo sheds in Tilbury as a store on a temporary basis. It was 21 shed and on the quayside adjacent to the berth, but yet again we were told that both berth and shed were likely to be pulled down for redevelopment. As we had heard this time and time again at the old Surrey Commercial Docks, and nothing had happened for years, it was not unreasonable to suppose that the system would still prevail. In any case there was no alternative.

We went alongside at Convoy's and took as much miscellaneous gear on board as we could accommodate. Every space below was filled and we carried a deck cargo too. When we went into the lock at Tilbury one of the lock staff was heard to say that the KJ looked like a marine jumble sale.

On Saturday March 21 we took her over the river into the floating dock and all of the underwater defects were dealt with, excluding the leak aft. We removed a piece of the copper sheathing but found nothing there, fitted a new transducer for the echo sounder and painted those parts of the sides that we had been unable to reach while she was afloat. All the underwater fittings were examined and pronounced OK.

On the weekend of April 25-26 1987, with a full crew of adult helpers, we made the last cruise before going into service; they were all occupied on various jobs for most of the time afloat. We went upstream to Convoy's again and took away most of what stores were still there - this ended our occupancy. They had been very good to us and we would have been very hard put to without their help.

On Friday May 1 we hoisted the Red Ensign and made our first ever voyage as the MSTS with a party of 1st Cuddington (Warspite) Sea Scouts, from Stoneleigh in Surrey. We had decided that, although the weekend was from p.m. on Friday, unless we had a long trip in view we would stay in the dock on Friday evening and leave on Saturday morning as soon as we could. In addition, some of the after-guard had to work on Friday and we could not reasonably ask them to forego half a day or a full day's work. Another thing was that, once in the river, there was nowhere we could get a berth out of the tideway. This would entail setting watch-keepers to ensure that nothing went wrong.

There was (and is) a Mission to Seamen clubhouse very close to the berth and they were agreeable to having the youngsters there for the Friday evening. There is table tennis, snooker and darts and also a small canteen where emergency rations such as Mars bars and the like can be bought. We impressed on them that they were only allowed there as a favour and we could not afford to fall out with the staff.

Just outside the dock there was a fish and chip shop which was very good and reasonably priced, but we did not give shore leave there as that part of Tilbury was a disaster area. Many of the shops were boarded up, there were several (rough) public houses and many of the street lights were broken. All of the time we were there we never once saw a road sweeper; once it had been a thriving port, but with the removal of the passenger ships it was a place to keep clear of.

The first cruise did not get off to a very promising start. At 0800 on Saturday I called the lock on the RT and asked if it was possible for us to lock out. I was told that the lock was being repaired and was out of order for 24 hours. In addition, they said they had never heard of us; they did not have a ship of that name in the dock and how long had we been there? I explained the position to them and was told that they would call back, which they did some ten minutes later - if we could be in the lock by 0700 they would let us out.

We got into the river with no trouble and headed downstream, the tide being with us. Everything we saw was new to the youngsters and also to most of us. Everybody wanted to get in the *wheel-house* so we made a roster to give them all a chance. Tilbury landing stage was the first landmark but unfortunately there was no ship on it. We explained there was usually a large cruise liner, commonly Russian or Greek, lying on the berth. The landing stage was a series of pontoons lashed together and the length is over 100 yards. There is a Customs and Police office on it, but that is only manned when there is a ship berthed. It is a nice berth for anybody to moor on if they are waiting for the tide, but the PLA are loathe to let any old body there. Sometimes we were lucky, but it depended on who was on duty at the time.

Tilbury Fort is nearby but the only thing visible from seaward is the top of the main door. Maintained by English Heritage, it has protected London's seaward approach from the 16th century through to the Second World War. Henry VIII built the first fort, and Queen Elizabeth I famously rallied her army nearby to face the threat of the Armada. From then on the only things of interest are the ships, seldom passenger-carrying ships but mostly a new breed of container ships. They usually look like a big box with a door at either end. The cargo is stacked into boxes that hold anything up to 500 tons each and as they are all one size they can be stacked up like bricks. They are often carried as deck cargo and with the accommodation right aft it is impossible for the crew to see anything near the bows.

There are some tankers, but not many, and another new breed of "sand suckers". These know the formation of the sea bed to a nicety and they have a very large scoop on one side. Tat is lowered down and it operates like a very large vacuum cleaner, sucking up sand or gravel and anything else that is on the bottom. The damage they do to fish stocks is incredible and any fish that is unlucky enough to get caught is blasted with sand and useless as food. It was one of these ships that sank the Marchioness. It is quite an event to see a proper ship with one or more funnels amidships and a foc'sle. These will soon become museum pieces.

Half a mile or so beyond Tilbury the river makes a right angle turn to the north, with the Essex marshes being on one side and the Kentish marshes on the other. For no apparent reason this area is called the Muckings and starboard green buoys mark the limits. At the top of Mucking Reach the river reverts to running due east to west. Here are to be found Shell Haven and Thames Haven, oil wharves with containers like overgrown mushrooms, holding millions of gallons of oil; that Hitler never managed to hit them seems miraculous. The river now runs east - west for some forty miles and it can be as rough here when the tide and wind oppose each other as anywhere around our coast. Wind against tide, the old salts will say, is trouble.

When we rounded Sea Reach the wind was on the bow and we hoisted fore and mizzen sails, more to provide something for the crew to do than to help us along. This was what most of them had come along for and they turned to with a will. There was a bit of motion and some of the crew began to look a bit green around the gills, but they claimed they were all right so we hoisted the mainsail. This was a different thing altogether but once they got it up the motion eased somewhat. It is always a pleasure to have a ship pass and know that somebody is watching and probably taking pictures. We were aiming at getting somewhere in the region of Southend at low water so, with time to kill, we dropped the sails and went alongside Southend Pier.

We were not very sure of what welcome to expect and we were always treated to some advice by the eternal fishermen who were always on the end. However, one of the pier staff took our lines and asked how long we would be staying. I told him that we expected to be about an hour and we were left in peace. We allowed the youngsters to go ashore so long as they stayed on the end and didn't go on the train. The Southend lifeboat used to be a seagoing boat and it lived in a hut at the top of a ramp on the pier head. It was always a pleasure to see it launched; with the crew on board a slip was tripped and the boat ran down to the end of the ramp creating a huge splash and an enormous wave. Now there is an inshore semi-inflatable, much the same as we carry, and it is lowered and hauled up with a short jib. The pier master came down to see us and he remembered us of old. He told us they charged ships for lying on the pier but that he hadn't seen us. He did suggest that if we wrote to the town clerk and told him who we were and what we did any dues would be waived. I did this and we are always made welcome.

With all our chicks safely aboard we crossed over to the south side of the river to the Medway Channel. The tide was just on the turn and we could not take any chances by crossing Medway Bank, so we rounded Medway Buoy, the outward end of the Channel. There is a wreck just clear of the end of the Channel and at low water there is quite a bit of it visible. She was a Liberty ship, The John Montgomery, and she was in a convoy during the war, loaded with ammunition and explosives of all kinds when she struck a mine. There must have been the biggest scatter of all time but for some reason she did not explode. She was taken in tow and got as far as the Medway where she foundered just outside Medway Channel on Grain Spit.

Naval divers have been down to look at her and without doubt many local people have had a look. Were she to one day explode where she is, unless there was a ship nearby it is unlikely that there would be any result other than a very large tidal wave and enough work to employ glazing firms on both sides of the river for five years. Suggestions have been made by pundits over the years of what to do, but in the end it was decided to leave her alone. A ring of wreck buoys have been put all round her and a permanent radar watch is kept. All vessels are enjoined not to enter the ring of buoys. She has been the subject of discussions, why was she towed in anyway; where was she going to be left if they had got her in; how long would she have remained afloat?

It is always easy to be wise after the event and while the salvage crew did a good and very dangerous job. It would have been so much easier if they had sunk her as far out to sea as they could, after the crew had been taken off. If she had reached an anchorage she would have provided more headaches than she has done where she is. Certainly both the Naval bases, Chatham and Sheerness, would never have let her get anywhere within their manor because she was far too dangerous. To the questions "Who would have unloaded her?" and "What would they do with the cargo supposing it was brought off?" there are no realistic answers. Obviously none of the cargo could have been used, whatever is was. In all probability it was fairly safe in that explosives on their own with no means of detonation are usually very stable, but nobody could say with certainty what stresses the cargo had been put to. Now she will remain where she is until the ebb and flow of Medway tides have dealt with the matter.

Garrison Point, once a fortress at the entrance to the Medway, came up. Here is where the first Sheerness dockyard, the smallest one in the Navy, used to be. It was the first yard to be scrapped and Sheerness was for some time a ghost town. Its whole reason for being was as a dockyard and every small shop in the small town was linked to the yard. Nowadays the whole place is transformed; the yard itself is almost always busy with two new berths having been built where the old pier used to be. There is also a berth that is right on the knuckle, a RO-RO berth; translated, this is a berth for "Roll-on-Roll-off" ferries. Ships thus called are getting very frequent where there is not enough room for a normal berth. They have doors at both ends and they berth where vehicles can run down a ramp and into the hull where they either berth or unload and then go out at the other end.

There is a profusion of buoys in the Medway, which is a very winding river carrying a lot of shipping. As heavy cruisers and aircraft carriers used to go up to Chatham there is obviously a deep water channel, but on the occasions when there is a yacht race in progress dozens of small yachts come down like enraged butterflies. They are all over the river and each one is concerned only with how the owner can gain a few feet on another craft; it is a wonder there are so few accidents, or to put it more correctly "unnecessary collisions".

Up to Bull Nose, where the main entrance to the dockyard used to be, there are few yacht moorings, but from then they are moored in lines, some in the middle of the river and some on one side or the other. Past Bull Nose the river makes almost a full circle, much like the Isle of Dogs in the Thames, and everything in that circle used to be a dockyard. Further up river there are two sharp turns to Rochester Bridge, and here there are small boat yards on both sides of the river. There is also a small public landing stage but it had a notice on it declaring that mooring was barred. When we asked Medway Radio where we could berth, they replied that there were no berths, but eventually we went alongside a Thames Barge that was moored to a buoy. We gave shore leave to all the crew, with strict orders that they were to be back on the jetty by 2200, from which we would pick them up with the ship's dinghy. They were all present and correct, and after we had provided them with a meal and a session of old salt's tales they finally gave up and went to sleep.

Next morning it was raining slightly and the shipping forecast was Thames Dover, wind NW force 6, moderating. Visibility good, rain showers. A later forecast was similar but gave the wind a NW force 6, gusting to force 7, with good visibility and rain showers. For once, with Monday being a Bank Holiday, we had a day in hand, so we decided to stay where we were; to be in the estuary with a possible force 7 from any quarter was no place for us if it could be avoided. The crew went ashore again, as did we, leaving a volunteer on board. Rochester is a nice place, very Dickensian, with a very big castle. Mr Dickens Senior was a clerk in the dockyard and Rochester makes the most of it.

Where young people are concerned they soon use up all of the attractions and ended up in a juke box shop; however they all said they enjoyed it! Its attraction to us was that it was about the only place in the estuaries where it was possible to get a berth that did not call for an anchor watch that was a reasonable distance from base.

On the next day, Bank Holiday Monday, the shipping forecast was: Thames, wind NW force 6, falling. Visibility good. Rain showers. We slipped at 0630 and ran the ebb tide down to Garrison Point with no problem. We waited about for an hour for the tide to turn and then ran up to Tilbury under fore and Mizzen only. We locked in at 1452 and were in our berth and all hands ashore at 1530.

This was the pattern for most weekends. Provided we could work it so we did not do too much punching the tide, we could always manage to berth safely somewhere at Rochester as we were very well known as a regular user of the Rivers Thames and Medway.

In that first year we carried 106 young people of both sexes and spent 12 weekends at sea with them. Tilbury dock became used to us and we managed to get the use of a hydraulic hoist if we had work to do aloft. The port manager said that he could not authorise the loan of the hoist; however, *if* we happened to find it near our berth and *if* we could find the keys and *if* we used it, he did not want to know! We never took the mickey by using this too much, and by no time we were on good terms with most of the dock personnel, especially the lock staff.

We used to tell them on a Friday evening that we would like to go out on the Saturday and arranged as far as possible to leave at the best time for them. On the return, if we called them up on channel 19 when we were off the landing stage we were always given a time to be off the lock and although sometimes we would have to wait outside for a ship to be unberthed or berthed, generally we locked in and out to our and their mutual satisfaction.

We asked Thames Radio if we should inform them of our movements in the river and were told that it would be in everyone's interest to do so. There are points on the river at which Gravesend Radio is called up, the norm being "Gravesend Radio, *Kenya Jacaranda* at Sea Reach 4, outward" (or inward as the case may be). The same applies in the Medway, albeit on channel 74 using buoys to notify positions.

On one occasion we were in the Medway Channel, going outwards and had notified Medway Radio at Garrison Point that we were going over to Thames Radio. As well as several small and medium coasters at anchor just outside the Channel we also saw a ship's lifeboat, apparently under oars. As far as we could see, there were two men in it with an oar apiece, one on each side. It was obvious that they were novices and there was a conversation going on between one of the anchored ships and Medway Radio. When the radio is on all the time you tend to hear all of the conversations as background noise, but once your own name is called you recognise it at once.

We heard Medway Radio say that one of the harbourmaster's craft was at Chatham and the other one was out of service. Then we heard our name called, asking if we had heard the conversation and could we help. Apparently two stewards from a coaster had decided to go for a spin in one of the lifeboats that had been put in the water to tighten up the hull. Having got into the boat and cast off they then found that the engine would not start. Having told Medway Radio that we would deal with it, we cut the engines and drifted up to the boat and gave a wee toot on the siren. They took our rope and we towed them back to the parent ship where we cast them off. We told Medway Radio that the wanderers had rejoined and the Master came on the air and thanked us. It would have been instructive to hear the comments when they got on board.

On another occasion we were inward bound in the Medway Channel approaching the Montgomery. There was a small cabin cruiser anchored just outside the Channel and while one of the fishermen stood up waved to us one of his companions let off a smoke flare. They obviously thought we were ignoring them but we had to come up into the wind to lower the mainsail; having done-that we came up to them to ask what was wrong.

They had been fishing for some hours and decided to call it a day when they found their battery was flat and they could not start their engine. They wanted to go to Lee, on the other side of the river, and we told Medway Radio that we were dealing with the problem. There would have been no question of declining to help - the unwritten rule of the sea is that help is never refused. We had decided to bring them alongside and put one of our batteries into her to start their engine and then put the battery back. It would have been possible but awkward, as our batteries weighed some 60 pounds each and they do not float; we could well have lost one of them. If that had failed we might have had to tow them into Sheerness, which was about the only place that they could get help.

At this point Medway One (the Harbourmaster's launch) chipped in; apparently they had seen us take our sails down and turn into the wind. In a matter of minutes they took over from us and took the cruiser in tow. We were grateful for this because if we had towed them across we would have missed the tide altogether.

The last cruise in 1987 was to Old Sun Wharf, a dry dock at Gravesend. We had taken as much gear as we could out of her and settled her over the dock. She dried out nicely and as soon as we could we got down into the dock and looked all around the hull. We could see nothing wrong at the stern end, which was a disappointment - we had hoped that there would be some evidence of the constant leak, but there was none.

We took both gearboxes and both screws out and left at 2300. On Saturday October 10 a small party went to Gravesend and took her back to Tilbury. She had been partly de-stored and this time we took the sails off and sent them to the sailmaker for inspection and winter storage. The yard had done several jobs that we were not able to do. They put in a very smart white line all round on the waterline and made up a sleeve to fit snugly over the end of the bowsprit. They had removed quite a bit of copper cladding, but this was to prove to be to no avail as they had not been able to trace the leak aft.

The first trip in 1988 was to be a landmark. We left Tilbury at 0100 Saturday April 30 with an all adult crew and ran right down to North Foreland. The tide was under us most of the way but we were not able to hoist any sail until we rounded the Foreland, not lowering it again until we were off of Ramsgate. The tide was against us now but we ran into Ramsgate outer harbour at 1230. All hands snatched a few hours sleep until 1630 when we left and headed to North Goodwin light vessel, then to South Goodwin, clearing there at 2100 hours. These lanes are new and mark the busiest sea lanes in the world. In effect they are "one way streets" for ships of all sizes and nationalities and they must be crossed at right angles; but despite the fact that a 24 hour radar watch is kept on them to see the rules are complied with, there are still collisions. We entered Calais Roads at 2200, downed all sail and entered the inner harbour and secured at 2300

The day was spent in Calais, with a run ashore to take advantage of the cheap goods on offer and to consume mussels and wine, and then back on board for a few hours sleep. Most of us felt that 24 hours in a bunk was not a bad prospect.

We were pleased to hear a reasonable weather report, although little up to a full storm warning would have kept us; leaving at 2345 we soon cleared the harbour, when all sail was set and the engines turned off. At 0300 the mizzen downhaul was fouling the radar bracket, but the sail was only lowered for some ten minutes and it was up again. We ran outside the Goodwins and picked up East Margate light at 0600. With the wind still held fair we ran from North Foreland right up to Sea Reach 6, when we notified Gravesend Radio of our homecoming.

The sails were lowered and stowed and, having contacted the lock, we were cleared to go straight in. As we had been flying the 'Q' flag, indicating that we had come from a foreign port and required Customs clearance, we were met by HM Customs Officers at the lock. It always arouses their curiosity when a yacht goes abroad and returns within 36 hours, but by good fortune both officers knew us and what we did and there was no complication. By 1430 we had berthed, feeling a mite harassed and eager to get home.

On Friday May 27 1988 we again went to Calais, but this time with a crew of youngsters. Unfortunately the wind was foul when we left Tilbury at 2115, but we set all sail and ran all the way to North East Goodwin light vessel by 0630. On Saturday we had to use the engines to Calais, which we reached at 1227. Customs clearance was a formality and shore leave was given to 2330. On the next day, Sunday, the weather was standard for a Bank Holiday, raining and blowing. The 1800 forecast for Thames Dover was wind SW, force 5 to 6, visibility good, with showers in the Dover area, wind gusting to force 5-7, possibility 8.

We lashed everything down and rigged life lines. We could not use the sails, and although even one would have steadied her up it was not to be. Monday 3rd May found us off North Foreland, with the shipping forecast the same as before. Once we had got round to the river we were able to use the sails until we reached Southend, lowering them and travelling on engines alone from there on. We berthed at 1415, and after Customs came and went so did we.

One thing we learnt from the two trips was that weatherwise we could never find a more seaworthy craft of her size, and provided she was not mishandled she would never let us down. The old Bo'sun used to say, "They might starve yer but they'll never drown yer".

A further six weekend trips were made, the usual run to Southend, Rochester and return. One trip with complications was on June 11 1988. We were in Rochester and the weather was not too good, with the forecast even less promising; wind NE, force 5-6, increasing, wind at Garrison Point 35 knots. However, whatever the weather, we had to go. When we passed No. 12 Buoy at 1221 the swell was uncomfortable, so we hoisted the foresail to try to ease the rolling. Having just made an attempt to get past Garrison Point, the port engine stopped and she would not answer the helm. By backing the foresail we managed to turn into the Medway again, where the rolling was less severe. We tried to pick up a buoy at Queensborough, but with only one engine it was hopeless. The fault was not with the engine but with the Bowden cable in the *wheel-house*, which had broken with the result that there was no means of controlling the engine revolutions. Luckily at Salt Pan Reach we just managed, by a fluke, to get a rope on a buoy after several attempts. We called Garrison Point on the radio with the message, "*Kenya Jacaranda* unable to round Garrison Point; we only have one engine. Can you give us sea and wind?" Reply: "Conditions same as when you tried before. You have a very clean bottom. What are your intentions?" Reply: "We are staying in the river. Thank you".

We ran on one engine back to Rochester, in the knowledge that not only could we get a mooring there but that there was easy access to the railway if we had to leave her. As it happened a Kent Police heavy launch went past en route to Maidstone, and we called her up. Having asked if they would inform the parents that the cruise was aborted and that the crew would be coming back early, they took the list and said the parents would be informed.

Half an hour later we were called up by Maidstone Police to say that our messages had been passed on. In conveying our thanks I added the International Police Association motto, which is in Esperanto: "Servo Par Amickeko" ("Service through Friendship". There was dead silence for a while, after which the radio operator said "Repeat please". Having duly done so I overheard him say "Listen to this Dick" before Dick said, "Come again please" There was then another long pause, after which he said "Oh yes, all right mate"! I shall never know whether or not he understood my Esperanto.

On Wednesday 15th June a small recovery party went to Strood with a new cable and brought her home. One pleasant thing was that the Youth Club concerned - Bexley Council for Racial Equality, declined to let the Society pay the rail fare for their party.

By the end of the year we had done 18 weekends, with a few variations, such as one trip when we went up the river Crouch to Pin Mill, a well known beauty spot. On another one we acted as guard ship for Gravesend regatta, which did not entail much trouble, but let us show the flag.

We were very worried about our store ashore, not only because 21 shed at Tilbury was very insecure but also because we knew that it was due to go. The doors were big sheets of corrugated iron on steel frames and it took a lot of man power to move them. There were several holes in the sides where lorries or yard vehicles had chewed lumps out and security was minimal. The actual berth for the ship also fluctuated, and we sometimes had to move her to some other berth for a few days. We were very lucky in that a member of the Society worked in the dock and he was adept at moving her single handed.

We tried to get the loan of a container from one of the shipping firms in the dock. When we tried Cunard they forwarded the letter to their head office, who were very definite in turning us down, but I was approached shortly afterwards by their manager at Tilbury who was very apologetic at the company's rejection and said that he would give us the use of a large container, but only on loan. He also said that it must not go out of the dock and we must not paint or alter any of the numbers on it. Nevertheless, this was a great help, especially as the yard manager said that he would put it anywhere we wanted. The PLA had to be consulted about it because the space that it occupied would be charged to the Society.

By this time we were accepted as part of the yard and any help that we asked for was seldom denied us. Despite the fact that we only got the container on loan, it is now "past its sell-by date" and it is now ours. We have fitted racks inside and it holds everything that we own, even if it is a tight fit.

In 1989, from April to October we were away for 24 weekends, being able to do so because we now had a second skipper We went to Shotley for a week for their festival and showed the ship off to other interested users of the sea.

The next year, 1990, we attracted the services of a third skipper, and now we needed more engineers. On the weekend July 13-15 we took the Beckton Youth Project, who made a most inauspicious start by being the first group to merit being banned from the Seamen's Mission on account of their general behaviour, together with their foul language. I told the leaders in no uncertain terms that this was the first time that any youth group had upset the Mission and we could not afford that. The group was sent back on board and were not let ashore. On Saturday the weather forecast was not too good but it did not merit staying in dock. We left at 0920 and as soon as we were clear KJ started pitching violently. To avoid having multiple cases of mal-de-mer we headed up river as far as Greenhithe, where we turned round and ran at half speed back to Tilbury Landing Stage, where the motion was reduced considerably, to the relief of the crew.

We parked for the night alongside a trot of barges in Gravesend Roads and having landed the crew on Gravesend Pier they all came back before the time we had allotted them. On Sunday the weather had moderated, although it was still not very warm. We ran down river as far as Southend Pier; we were conscious of the fact that the crew had come for a weekend sail, but that was about the best we could do because of the weather. We berthed on the end of the pier and let them all go ashore, telling them to be back on board by 1300 so as to be able to run up with the tide.

By 1315 they were all back except for four lads, one of whom was a leader. At 1330 one of the remaining leaders went ashore to try to find them but without success. By 1415 they were still absent and we made enquiries of Southend Police, thinking that the worst had happened, but there was no knowledge of them. The senior leader went ashore to find them and return them by train, with sufficient money to pay their fare, and we slipped our mooring. Just as we cleared the pier and were full ahead for Tilbury, the Harbourmaster's launch that had been moored on the pier with us came on the air and said that our four heroes had arrived. We asked them if they would run the miscreants out to us as we were already committed to punching the tide and they agreed. There was no excuse for them but they were laughing as if it was a good joke. I was only sorry that we did not have the time to give them a bit of rough weather to dampen them down a bit.

We told the leaders that we would not entertain another trip for that group, which was all we could realistically do. As it was, we had an hour and a half punching the tide and docked at 1820.

On the August Bank Holiday 1990 weekend there was an open day in Tilbury Docks and we were asked to be there as an attraction. We were only too pleased to be able to do something for Tilbury, who had been very good to us. We dressed the ship overall and did seven or eight trips "round the harbour" with a lot of people on board. We sold some 'T' shirts and photographs of the ship and netted £120 for the day, which came in very handy. The manager of the yard was there and made a point of coming on board. He was very interested in how we got our money and we told him that 50% of it came from the London Boroughs Grants Unit at Richmond and the other 50% was down to us. We explained the various means we used and, as he did not appear to be making any offers, I suggested to him that, to the Port of Tilbury, our monthly payment for the lock fees for the room that our container took up was hardly worth the trouble and paperwork it involved. He hesitated a minute then gave a little smile and said "Strike while the iron's hot, eh Steve? – OK, No charges as of today'."

That was a big boon for us, and took at least a little of the worry from the Treasurer. The charge for the container was based on the actual size of the land that the container sat on in square feet, multiplied by the number of days it was there. Another bonus was that we were getting our diesel oil free. We used to phone the office in the dock and arrange for delivery by a bowser (a tanker lorry) and it would be delivered and signed for and that was the end of it.

The question of privatising the dock was on the agenda again. Tilbury wanted it but Customs and Excise would not entertain a dock being policed by a private firm. The PLA police numbers were being eroded all the time. At one time they numbered several thousand and policed all the docks on the north of the river, East and West India, St Katharine Docks, the Royal group, Millwall, London and Tilbury and on the south side the Surrey Commercial Docks.

Their authority extended for half a mile outside the docks and co-operation between the two forces, Metropolitan and PLA, was a hundred percent. The first to go was the smallest, St Katharine Docks, then the Surrey followed by the whole group on the North side, an area of several hundred acres, with Tilbury ending up as the only dock still policed by the PLA. They still were the authority for the Harbourmaster's duties and buoyage. From having a Chief Police Officer, Chief Superintendent, Superintendents, Chief Inspectors, Inspectors, and Constables, the Force has been steadily whittled away until they have one Chief Inspector, four sergeants and thirty constables. Essex Police have been approached with a view to them taking over the dock, but they don't want to know, so at the moment it is stalemate.

Customs and Excise also have a lot to do with the river and its users and they do, of course, have a lot of liaison with the police. They are also much more active where ships are concerned. We had an example of this when, on returning from a trip to Calais, we had come up the river flying 'Q' flag, a yellow meaning "I am coming from abroad and I require free pratique [permission to use a port]". Nobody is allowed ashore until this has been given by a Customs Officer. Customs log all ships leaving and entering the country and on this occasion an officer had obviously noticed that the KJ was returning from abroad, having only left on the Saturday.

The Duty Officer came out in the launch and asked to see the log and he and two Customs Officers came with us to our berth. At first they did not have much to say, but when they saw the very young crew they asked what we did. When we reached our berth there was a rummage crew waiting for us. A rummage crew is a team of Customs officers who specialise in finding every possible hiding place on a ship and, sometimes, when their information is good, they will almost wreck a ship in their hunt. Some of them knew the boat and how long it had been on the river and the officer in charge said to me "We are very interested in a boat like yours going over to France and back again after a very brief stop!" They found nothing.

Whilst all this was going on the ship was still in business and was away most weekends. We had resolved that we would get to the bottom of this constant leak aft and to that end we had made a booking with Ramsgate Marine for November. This firm had the use of three slips in Ramsgate and two of them would take the ship, the third was too small.

We had been to Rochester four times and had spent a week in Shotley, where they had an annual sailing regatta. We could not take any active part in most of the various events, as she as too cumbersome for the sort of races they held and there were not many other events where such a craft could participate. It was better to have people visiting her who could spread the gospel about a Brixham Trawler being a sail training vessel. Of course, of the many people who visited her, most if not all of them were already confirmed sailing types.

Chapter 9 - Endless Repairs

At the end of the cruising weekends we took her to Ramsgate with a defect list and left her. I went to South Africa for a month and when we were collected by my son Roger from Heathrow he told me that she was still there. Knowing his macabre sense of humour I did not take it seriously until he said that he wasn't joking. He didn't know the whole story so I was anxious to find out what had happened.

She had been slipped and, once all of the work we wanted done had been dealt with, she was put back in the water waiting to go home. On Saturday October 6 1990 she set off home, but after an hour's run there appeared to be more water inside than there was outside and the pumps were unable to cope. She was taken back to Ramsgate and left once again in the care of Ramsgate Marine. The following day, Sunday, she was making water so fast that she was put into the inner harbour with a portable pump on a float switch in her bilge.

The firm had tried to locate the leak in various ways, none of which had managed to trace it. The firm had bookings for the two slips and the traditional annual holiday, which meant that nothing could be done until January. In the meantime she was being pumped out three or four times a week..

I went to Ramsgate with the engineer to meet our new surveyor, Mr Cormack. The surveyor we had with dealt for years was not on the approved list for the new Code of Practice (for sailing vessels) and Mr Cormack was the nearest who was.

The ship gave the impression that she had been sunk and raised for salvage. She was a very poor old lady, water everywhere. Floor boards had been pulled up in an effort to locate the leak, but as she had some thirty tons of iron ballast in her it was all very hit and miss. Mr Cormack was very curious about her history and her present predicament and appeared to be sympathetic to our cause. However, nothing could be done until she was out of the water and he asked to be informed when she was.

On January 3 1991 she was duly slipped and water was leaking everywhere, but we expected this as we knew from experience that this always happened – it was mainly water trapped between the copper sheathing and the hull. Mr Cormack went over the hull and hammered everywhere hoping to find a place where there was bad timber, but the whole hull gave off a dull thump instead of a hard echo. When he asked us when the copper had last been inspected we told him we had never interfered with it as long as it kept the water out. In his view it was customary for a sheet to be removed every time she was surveyed; we could only plead ignorance. He wanted us to take a strip of copper off both sides of the bow and stern from the waterline to the keel and another strip amidships and then get back in touch with him. However, he told us that the copper was not serving any useful purpose in home waters, only being of use in tropical waters.

At this point Mr Barsley, the yard foreman, who was aware of our limitations, said that if we liked we could remove the copper ourselves at weekends and he would give us the use of the slip. In his experience there was no easy way to do it, that it was merely a matter of brute force and plenty of ignorance, coupled with judicial use of a club hammer and chisel. We were very pleased to do this and arranged to start the first weekend, January 4-6, with a party of 14 volunteers working from staging which had been erected all around the hull. That first day was by far the worst day of all with the wind coming off the sea; it was impossible to work on the windward side for fear of being blown off. Fortunately we could concentrate all our efforts on the other side, but even that was fraught with danger because of the blustering wind, and although we begrudged the time it took we rigged safety lines.

That first weekend we cleared a fairly large area on the starboard, the lee side; on the forefoot there were several planks that had rot in them far too big to even *think* of letting pieces in. Peter Barsley came on the Sunday to see how far we had got and he told us that, if we asked the surveyor to come and give an opinion, he would certainly tell us to get the lot off. On the face of it we agreed, and we were able to take a token strip off on the Sunday. Peter Barsley said that if we lumped the scrap copper into manageable pieces he would get the boy to put it on the lorry and he would take it to the scrap dealer. He also said we might as well make use of the amenities on offer, hot water, showers if we wanted them and the usual offices!

By the end of the fourth weekend we had cleared not only all the old copper, but also the new that had been put on at Maldon. All of the area around the rudder and the two screws had been removed each time she was out of the water in an attempt to locate the leak. This had been done carefully, in order to save as much of the copper as possible, but we could never save it all and we always had to buy some more.

What we had never done, never even thought of doing, was work on the area where the longitudinal planks met the stern post and were affixed to it. Here, on both sides, there was not an inch of caulking! This was the place in the hull where the caulking should have been of the highest quality, yet not an ounce of hemp or other caulking medium had been used. The yard at Maldon had relied on the copper sheathing to hide their shoddy work. There, for all the world to see, was the worst piece of malpractice of the lot. We took several pictures of this from all angles and told Peter Barsley that, if it went our way, we might want his testimony. In the event it was not required.

Over four weekends we cleared the whole hull, using a high pressure hose to remove the odd bits and pieces of light canvas that had been put between the copper and the hull and then tarred. Then all the caulking had to be hardened down and all the nail holes plugged with a special stopper, which was supplied by Peter Barsley.

We cannot speak too highly of the help we got from the that yard; most shipyards would not allow the owner or his or her representatives on a vessel in their yard, let alone give them the run of the yard at weekends. When I asked Peter Barsley how much he thought we had saved by the work we had done he told us that if his men had stripped the copper the wages bill would have been in the thousand pound bracket. In addition, as well as saving that considerable sum, we got just over £400 from the sale of the copper.

I told him how much we had paid for the work that was done (or, more to the point, wasn't done) at Maldon, and the treatment we had received there, he said that if their yard had done the job, in his estimation it would have cost only *half* of what we had been charged, and from what he had seen we would have had a far better job at the end of it. One more example of being wise after the event.

It was not long afterwards that the hull repairs were finished. She had two coats of preservative paint on the bottom, two coats of boot topping and a new white load line. By the weight of the copper we took off she should have been a bit higher in the water!

I asked the yard for a rough estimate of the bill we would have to pay. Whatever it was going to be, it was a racing certainty that we would not have enough money to meet it. Peter had already reached that conclusion on what I had told him about our circumstances. He told us that it was a hard and fast rule that no ship left the yard without the bill having been settled as they had been caught once and the manager had said, "Never again". It would be in the region of £19,000.

We had estimated around £15,000, but we had nothing like that. Anyway, Peter told us that we would have to see the Managing Director, who came down about twice a month but generally without any prior warning. As an afterthought he asked whether we had done anything about harbour and slip dues, but we hadn't; we would have to find another £900 for that.

The Treasurer reported to Peter Harding and I that our total cash in hand was £9,400 and that was really scraping the barrel. After a lot of thought we decided to make an appointment to see the M.D. of the firm and throw ourselves on his mercy, subsequently seeing him at the firm a week later. He had already been told the position so that when we were introduced to him he said, "You have got yourselves into a real state haven't you?" We told him it wasn't so much a case of getting ourselves into this state as being pitch-forked into one. He had not been told about our stay at Maldon and when we told him exactly what had happened he thawed quite a bit. He said, "If we let you out of here will you promise to pay?" Of course we would, but it might take a while; on that promise and a shake of hands a deal was made.

He then asked about the ship, where she had come from and how we got her; I told him about the Sea Cadets, how it had got increasingly difficult to run her and how the MSTS had been formed as a Registered Charity to continue in the same way. He had had something to do with Sea Cadets some years ago, at Trafalgar Square, and had met a Lt Commander Rowe, who was also known to me: I recalled that he had what I though was a most unusual way of introducing his wife. He used to say, "This is the lady I live with". Were I to use that phrase to introduce my wife I could have guaranteed a very fast and to-the-point retort. He remembered that himself and thought that perhaps it was one of those odd Naval customs! That was the first and last time we ever saw the M.D., and to this day I cannot remember his name.

We paid our debt for the slip and the stay in the marina, which left us with a bill of £17,500 to pay. Having paid £9,000, which left us just solvent, Peter Harding got £2,000 from a benefactor, we got an interest free loan of £2,000 and then started an all-out appeal for help. It was not a good time to ask for money but bits and bobs came in and we finally cleared the debt some 18 months later.

We were still left with "The Safety of Small Commercial Sailing Vessels - Code of Practice". We told the Association of Sail Training Organisations, who administer the Code, that we would not be able to complete the whole thing in under two years and told them why. One of the things they required was that the engines had to be totally enclosed, so our shipwright Peter Aldrich enclosed them in what amounted to a large cupboard, constructed of one inch marine ply lined with foil.

Before this was constructed there were two entrances to the engine compartment. One was via a hatch and a steel ladder just for'ard of the mizzen mast, with the other via the starboard aft (Engineer's) cabin - a door had been cut in the bulkhead to allow access. This had, up until then, always been the way in and out, but with the new Code of Practice that had to go so that the only access was the hatchway. This meant that the poor old engineer's life would be in danger when he had to go into the engine room in a beam sea, or when the hatch was opened in a heavy sea and a big lump of water was dumped through the hole!

Work went on all the time on the ship, mostly at weekends although some volunteers managed to work during the week. Doors were fitted, all the lights were wired in, the hull was painted, stowage space was built, both for the bunks and for the galley area. The ship was dry docked twice at Gravesend both to allow surveys and to enable us to do necessary work that was not possible when she was afloat. This included such tasks as moving the transducer for the echo sounder, checking the rudder fastenings, striking in the waterline, trying to trace the source of the leak aft, etc. etc; all things that should have been done at Maldon. Our finances were at an all time low.

We had to pay dock and harbour dues, dry docking, fuel and lubricating oil and almost all the material required for completion; the only thing that came free was the labour! The whole water system was overhauled and a lot of electric wiring had to be changed; the mizzen mast had to be extended because the peak of the mainsail fouled the radar scanner; the skylight was fixed and caulked, the worst of the deck leaks was payed and we made and fitted a derrick for launching and recovering the tender.

There were still teething troubles, the most persistent being the number of leaks in the deck which we were continually trying to stop by caulking and paying the worst areas. Additionally, the ever present leak right aft was always a worry and a cause for anxiety. It never stopped and every time the ship was docked a section of the new copper sheathing in that region was taken off, but nothing was ever found. At one stage grease was injected from the inside but this had no effect when she went back in the water. When the ship was in the dock at Gravesend we asked the shipwright there to give us an estimate. He said that the only was to deal with it was to go over the whole deck and this they could not do unless we could leave the ship at Gravesend for a week. This we were unable to do because of (a) cost and (b) because we did not have the time.

Eventually, in the winter of 1989 we got a firm from Rochester, Peninsular Marine Services, to give us an estimate. After seeing the job Mr Spratt, the manager, suggested that they were unable to give a firm quote as there was no way of knowing whether the caulking seams lined up. The suggestion was that they did a week's work on the deck, starting for'ard at a weekly rate of £350, and see how much work they got done.

This was done and we were impressed by the amount of caulking and paying that they did and we agreed to finish the job at that rate. They did an excellent job but the final tally came to just over £3,000. I asked Mr Spratt to give me a report on what he found, his report said, verbatim; "There were several places where the black glue or pitch was less that 1/4" thick in the seams. There were three different ages of oakum indicating that these seams have not been caulked in the same period. Some of the deck seams have gaps up to 1/4" wide on the UNDERSIDE of the planks and there was no oakum at all in most of the butt ends between planks. There had been different types of caulking in the seams including rope, oakum, cotton and mud."

In addition the hatches and skylight had not been set into the deck, but on top of it, so as there was no way of caulking them quadrant was set all round them and glued.

***

At this stage, Steve's story abruptly ends. Roger Stevens has, from the logs and other sources of information, compiled a very brief history of Kenya Jacaranda post-Steve.

The Kenya Jacaranda after Steve
by Roger Stevens

Information about the subsequent years can to a degree be gleaned from the logs, but these are merely factual and some of them are missing anyway. There is a little bit of humour to be had from them and it is worthy of note that the handwriting is frequently dire!
Trips continued, seemingly uneventfully, on most weekends through 1989. There is one note in the log for the trip on 6th August:

> Party ashore for fresh water; captured by local hostile publican, allowed to escape after giving him money and being made to drink strange coloured water. This was in Southend!

Another 24 trips, mostly with youth groups, were achieved between April and October.
In 1990 it was noted: "Ron Thompson (bos'n) refused a nightcap". Anyone who knew Ron will be well aware that this was unprecedented. On another trip the log records "Helmsman watching helicopter – off course".

There were another 20 trips running right into November 1990 when KJ was taken to Ramsgate Marine slipway for some work to the hull and stripping of the copper sheathing on the hull at weekends by members. She remained in Ramsgate until 22 March 1991 when the crew brought her home to Tilbury.

That year it was noted in the log: "Error by Paul Ellis PC 123 compounded by cabin boy Aldrich". No explanation was given - perhaps someone was wasting paper. There were a total of 15 trips, the highlight seeming (from the log) to have been the cooking of a Spotted Dick!

On one trip in 1992 the log records: "1815 Thames barge making for same buoy – won by 2 bowsprit lengths. Steve would have been proud".

A Brixham trip in August showed that £2,000 was raised from visitors during the two-day stay. The son and widow of the original owner and an original crew member's widow were noted as visitors. This was an extended trip with crew changes en route. It is to be noted that Calais seems to have been on a direct route from Brixham to Tilbury! They called in there on the way back.

The last group of the year was to St Katharine Docks. A note in the log reports: "Police aboard, no arrests. Sleep maintenance. No drinking. Dinner Beef Bourguignon avec vino! " There were a total of 21 trips that year.

In 1993 there were 18 trips including one extended voyage to France. A note in log reported that: "One of crew (name withheld) advised to give up half his sex life. Remainder of crew decided the half he had to give up was talking about it!"

In 1994 there were 26 trips including one of 12 days to Cherbourg, Guernsey, Jersey and Poole, taking 12 days and covering nearly 500 miles. One trip has notations against crew names: "Assistant Admiral's mate (undercover), Accommodation services Manager (Loos), Ship's pet, Whitstable Gogo dancer, barnacle picker, window cleaner" That must have been an interesting trip!

The following year there were 12 trips before an extended Brixham trip. Leaving Poole on 23 August on the return trip *Kenya Jacaranda* went aground on a mud bank. Efforts to refloat her were in vain and eventually the rudder post was broken and she was towed to Poole quay. The resulting repairs are not recorded in the log book but initially the plan was for her to be slipped and a new post fitted by a shipyard. However, the Royal Marines who are based in Poole like a challenge and their divers managed to remove the rudder, drop it to the sea bed, fit a new post and re-attach the rudder. In September she was brought home and a further five trips were undertaken.

The year 1996 had a short sailing season with a total of twelve trips. These included extended trips to Holland and Belgium and another to France. In 1997 seven trips were logged up to August when the log was full. Those for the years to 2003 are sadly missing.

For some years our patient surveyor had been warning that, unless we could develop a rolling renovation plan, he would be forced to limit our sailing range or refuse us the necessary licences to allow us to continue sailing with youth groups. We had a quote to re-plank the starboard side and the Excelsior Yard in Lowestoft was contracted . An estimate of £50,000 was agreed and we somehow managed to accumulate this vast sum. Accordingly, in 2001 she was delivered. The shipwrights were from Brixham, men expert in working on these ships. We managed to secure accommodation for them in a holiday camp.

After the work had commenced it soon became clear that the extent of the rot was not merely limited to the planks: the frames also needed replacement. Our £50k estimate became £93k and once the work was completed we were left with a debt of £43k. The work took three months, with the hardworking Devon men working twelve days continuously and then taking two days off. When the work was completed KJ was reintroduced to the water.

It is testimony to the standard of the work that there was barely any seepage of water through the new planks, even though they had not yet 'taken up'. Another problem was then encountered; the traditional ballast in Brixham Trawlers was concrete contained in the bilges between the two skins. Our surveyor was not keen to replace the concrete but when she was refloated she listed several degrees. For the return to Tilbury this was overcome by lashing about twenty water barrels along the side to counterbalance the loss of ballast.

Once back in Tilbury we bought six tonnes of railway line which had been cut into short lengths; this was installed in the bilges, under the floor and the bunks, to make up for lost ballast.

In late 2002 a further trip to Lowestoft was undertaken for a survey needed for a National Lottery application and some repairs. The return trip from Lowestoft is labelled 'The Trip of the Damned' in the log, a crew of four in January 2003 in an unheated ship. One note says: "Egg butties, coffee and snow"! There were numerous minor problems dealt with en route and the log notes seventeen hours at sea before arriving at Tilbury.

In May of that year (2003) an extended Brixham trip was undertaken, with much painting work being done on the way down. KJ competed in the Trawler Race, not winning but being awarded the Concours D'Elegance for the best presented ship. The crew was changed for the return; it seems from the log that the only food left on board was eggs!

A further eight trips were completed that year; notes made in the log on one trip during anchor watch included "We really had fun, need sleep, saw cow jumping over the moon, dolphins and flying fish. Bacon butties were good. Saw a flying saucer. Snoring coming from all over the boat. 0500 sunrise, where's my sleeping bag?"

In 2004 the first trip of the year was to Lowestoft for a few repairs. She stayed there for two weeks until delivery back to Tilbury. That year a further seven short trips are recorded.

The following year one trip was completed before a voyage to Brixham was started but quickly aborted due to adverse weather. A further thirteen trips were completed, a final one being abandoned due to the skipper being ill.

The log entries end in 2006, the only trip recorded being to the Slip at Woolwich . By this time the debt from the Lowestoft refit was almost paid off but the effort to raise this sum had stopped any build-up of reserves to allow other work to be planned and all energy had seeped out of the efforts to find new sources of income.

In 2007, at an Extraordinary General Meeting of the MSTS, a proposal to 'wind up' the Society was debated, voted upon and agreed: the KJ was returned to her owner, Roger Stevens. Efforts to find a new home for her went on, but finding anyone with the resources and time to undertake a project of this size is, to say the least, difficult.

She continued to sail but for a decreasingly small amount of time. The money to keep her up to standard to be used for sail training failed to manifest itself and she gradually fell into disrepair, spending much of her time tied up at Tilbury. Ownership of the *Kenya Jacaranda* was transferred from Steve and Peter Harding in January 1998, her ownership ultimately passing into the hands of Steve's son Roger Stevens, who became the sole owner in November 2008. The MSTS was wound up August 2007. Ownership was later transferred to *Kenya Jacaranda* Heritage Sailing in 27 August 2009.

***

On 9 January 2010 at 1100, the Harbourmaster at Tilbury noticed that she was listing. His deputy notified both the police and skipper and engineer Paul Ladyman at around 1300 that she was definitely sinking.

Crew member Gerry Goldner arrived at around 1330 by which time she had submerged and was resting on the bottom. There was a 10 degree list to starboard away from the dock wall. The shore power lead was connected but it was impossible to check if there had been a supply as the socket on the boat was underwater.

As there were signs of diesel in the water, which it was assumed was coming from vents on the fuel tanks, the dock master arranged a water boom around her. It was not possible to board her as the water came to the top of the guard rails and she was 5 feet below the dock.

The situation was discussed with Port Harbour authorities. Crew members started arriving to help - Alan Bray at around 1400 followed by Mick Shirley at around 1430. Using his ladder to board, Mick got ropes around masts and tightened shore lines. It was hoped that this would prevent her from sliding down the mud when the water level dropped and falling on her side. He also lashed down some loose spars and planks.

By 1530 no further movement of vessel was noticed. The dock water level was around normal maximum at that time. Tilbury Port advised making contact with PLA salvage - they were familiar with working in the Port.

Raising the KJ was scheduled for 9 January. Tilbury Docks agreed that they could lower the water level by about a foot. Two large pumps were hired which could pump 3000 gallons per hour each. A team of old MSTS members who had heard of the disaster assembled and, working in freezing water about 2' deep, managed to block the various hatches (hammering in nails under freezing water isn't easy!) Pipes were lowered into the hull and the pumps started. Nothing happened for quite some time; then, after about 20 minutes, she started to lift and slowly returned to the surface.

Below decks was filthy; the surveyor who was present supervised the pumping of large amounts of clean water throughout the hull. The Engineer (Paul Ladyman) and the surveyor managed to remove the injectors from the engines, drain them and fill them with oil. Obviously the electrics, starter and alternators were wrecked but the following week Paul managed to get one, then the other engine running again.

It was the way the team came to the rescue that started the thought that, if a new organisation could be formed, the best thing for the future of the KJ would be for her to be 'gifted' to that body. None of the owners have ever thought of KJ as 'theirs' - they have considered themselves to have been custodians of a piece of history.

Thus the *Kenya Jacaranda* Heritage Sailing (KJHS) came into being. KJHS is now a registered charity and its members have undertaken regular maintenance to ensure KJ is, at the very least, stable, while others are undertaking the unenviable task of fundraising.

Further information on KJHS can be obtained from the new website:

www.kenyajacaranda.org

This story is included as a supplement - it details one of many times when the future of the *Kenya Jacaranda* was in jeopardy.

The Tall Ships Race - 1968

Harwich to Kristiansand, Norway

By Leading Seaman Martin T Daniels of the Lytham St Anne's Sea Cadet Corps

At 0930 on Monday August 5 1968 the *Kenya Jacaranda* slipped her moorings at Harwich. We were in the Class A race, which started at 1000. To a bugle call, we made our way towards the North Sea towards Kristiansand, which is on the southern tip of Norway. The wind was force 1 - 2 from ENE and when we rounded the Beach End Buoy the boat would not point to windward as well as other newer boats. Instead, we headed NNE at about 4 knots towards the *Sunk* lightship and the Shipwash Buoys.

We were only 16 miles from Harwich and had been at sea for 8 hours when we abandoned our fight with the tide and dropped anchor just east of the Buoy. We stayed at anchor until 2200 when the wind had changed to NE force 2 and the tide had slackened. Steering 085° we made 4 knots all night until once more the tide caused us to drop anchor at 0630. After 20 hours of sailing we were still only 50 miles from Harwich, 30 miles off Orford Ness. Once the tide had dropped we slipped anchor once more and sailed at 3 knots on a course of 340° towards Lowestoft. We were forced to drop anchor once again until at midnight we steered on a course of 100° for 4 hours followed by a tack of 350° for a further 4 hours.

At this point, at 0800 on 7 August the Skipper, Lt-Commander Morin-Scott started the port engine and steered a course of 100° with a tack of 350° until 1900 the following day, when the wind changed to northerly, after which we steered 050° and made 6 knots.

Early on the Saturday morning the wind eased to NW force 3 and we managed to steer a course of 035° straight for Kristiansand. With 250 miles to go we were half way but ploughing through the heavy seas at speeds of up to 8 knots, by midnight we were 150 miles away.

On the Sunday the wind eased - however, this was the lull before the storm. By 1200 the wind was force 6 - 7 and a small leak opened by the heavy seas had made us ship water. Over the next 3 hours the wind rose to force 8 and swells of up to 35 feet were looming all around.

The crew of 26 was kept busy either baling or pumping the water from the hull. A bucket chain was formed to expedite the baling while, in the Captain's quarters, four of the crew manned the hand-pump.

By 1800 things had got even worse. Heavy seas had broken our make-shift repairs to the starboard exhaust pipe and even more water was pouring in through there. By 2300 it was obvious that water was coming in quicker than we could get it out and in the engine-room it was waist-high.

A white stand-by flare was fired to attract the Norwegian frigate which we had been led to believe was on its way to escort us - in fact it never arrived. This was followed 15 minutes later by two red distress flares and a *Mayday* call was made over the radio. Shortly after this our generators failed as they were under water, so the radio was now out of action and so we fired a further two distress flares - almost immediately three ships appeared - two Norwegian cargo boats and a Danish passenger liner.

At 0200, escorted by the three ships and a helicopter which had by then arrived, we entered the sheltered waters off the Norwegian coast and were able to make an impact on the vast amount of water we had taken aboard by baling. By 0500 we were just about dry and the helicopter and two of the ships withdrew, leaving us in the care of the one of the cargo vessels.

After following the Norwegian coast for several hours the cargo vessel left us and at 0700 we sighted land - an hour later we could see Kristiansand Harbour. At this stage the Skipper ordered all hands to clean the ship and revert to "Bristol Fashion" after our night's battle with the elements. The crew then dressed in full Blues in preparation for entering harbour.

Throughout, the morale of the crew, mostly boys, like me, of 16, remained high. The entire ship's company had been completely calm and cheerful with no sign of panic. That being said, we were more than relieved when we took a tow for the last few miles by a Royal Norwegian gunboat.

At 0930 on Monday 12 August - my 16th birthday - seven days after leaving Harwich the *Kenya Jacaranda* sailed proudly into Kristiansand Harbour to the sound of hearty cheers from the crews of the other boats in the race.